TO

....

FROM

....

DATE

....

SANCTUARY IN THE *Psalms*

KJV

DaySpring

A Sanctuary in the Psalms

Second Edition, February 2022

Published by:

DaySpring

21154 Highway 16 East
Siloam Springs, AR 72761
www.dayspring.com

The Holy Bible, King James Version

Produced with the assistance of Peachtree Publishing Services.

Cover Design by: Greg Jackson of thinkpen.design

Printed in China
Prime: J7431
ISBN: 978-1-64870-417-8

TABLE OF CONTENTS

INTRODUCTION

Thy way, O God, is in the sanctuary:
who is so great a God as our God?
—Psalm 77:13

The book of Psalms is filled with words that express a heart's deepest sorrows, unfulfilled longings, intense fears, and emphatic praise of our Creator. Throughout the 150 psalms, God is described as a refuge, a shelter, and a hiding place. In him we find our sanctuary—a place of unconditional love and safety in his holy presence.

A Sanctuary in the Psalms helps readers engage with the psalms and find their sanctuary in God through its emphasis on nine themes highlighted throughout the text:

- ***Peace:*** When external turmoil threatens your inner stability, seek peace that can only come from standing in God's presence. *"I will both lay me down in peace, and sleep: for thou, Lord, only makest me dwell in safety" (Psalm 4:8).*

- ***Comfort:*** When the struggles of life overwhelm you with heartbreak or discouragement, receive God's comfort from the words of the psalmists. *"Thou shalt increase my greatness, and comfort me on every side" (Psalm 71:21).*

- **Hope:** When discouragement rains down on you, find hope in God's promises for you. *"Be of good courage, and he shall strengthen your heart, all ye that hope in the* LORD*" (Psalm 31:24).*

- **Strength:** When you feel weak and unable to keep going, God's strength will move you forward. *"The* LORD *is my light and my salvation; whom shall I fear? the* LORD *is the strength of my life; of whom shall I be afraid?" (Psalm 27:1).*

- **Gratitude:** When you battle discontentment, acknowledge God's goodness to you and cultivate a heart of thankfulness for all he is and all he does in your life. *"Sing unto the* LORD, *O ye saints of his, and give thanks at the remembrance of his holiness" (Psalm 30:4).*

- **Rest:** When you feel overwhelmed or troubled, seek God's Word and rest in his presence and in his sovereignty over your life. *"Therefore my heart is glad, and my glory rejoiceth: my flesh also shall rest in hope" (Psalm 16:9).*

- **Joy:** When you are overcome by sorrow, find joy in your everlasting relationship with your Creator. *"Thou wilt shew me the path of life: in thy presence is fulness of joy; at thy right hand there are pleasures for evermore" (Psalm 16:11).*

- **Grace:** When you are faced with your failures, be reminded of God's grace in your life—his forgiveness and unconditional love for you. *"He hath made his* *wonderful works to be remembered: the LORD is gracious and full of compassion"* (Psalm 111:4).

- ***Renewal:*** When your heart feels heavy, receive encouragement from God's promises of renewal and restoration. *"Create in me a clean heart, O God; and renew a right spirit within me"* (Psalm 51:10).

Our desire is that you will connect more deeply to the words in the psalms through this book. As you navigate the nine themes highlighted throughout *A Sanctuary in the Psalms*, enter God's sanctuary and allow his Word to revitalize your heart, your home, and your life.

PSALMS

INTRODUCTION

The book of Psalms is an Old Testament book of the Bible, found between the books of Job and Proverbs. It is sometimes referred to as a Psalter, a Latin church term meaning a book of Psalms used for church or devotional use. This could be considered somewhat of an early church hymnal.

Author: Unlike many other books in the Bible, the book of Psalms was written by more than one author. Some of the well-known authors include David, Solomon, and Moses.

- **David** is the most commonly known author. He wrote more psalms than any other author. He penned 75 of the 150 chapters that make up the Psalter. Although he is named as the author of Psalm 73, it is widely accepted by Christian scholars that he also wrote Psalm 2 and Psalm 95. David's psalms are often emotional and are marked with his honest feelings about his relationship with God through various trials and tribulations. David's psalms span many major events in his life, from when David fled from Absalom and then again later from Saul to when he had an affair with Bathsheba and had her husband killed on the battlefield.

- **Asaph**, a singer and seer in David's court, wrote twelve psalms. Asaph is also mentioned in the books of I Chronicles and II Chronicles as the chief of the tribe of Levi, where he and his brothers are appointed to sing songs to the Lord (see I Chronicles 16:4–7). Although in the biblical text Asaph's twelve psalms are attributed to him, it's possible that either one of his descendants wrote them or that he transcribed the psalms as David dictated the message.

- **The sons of Korah** wrote eleven psalms. The sons' story begins in Numbers, where their father and the rest of his tribe challenged Moses and Aaron and are swallowed up by the earth (see chapter 16). Thus, for the sons this is a redemption story—turning away from the history of their past and instead turning to God. Many of their psalms are marked with exclamations of praise to God.

- **Solomon** wrote Psalm 72 and Psalm 127. Solomon is better known for his contributions to Proverbs, Ecclesiastes, and Song of Solomon.

- **Heman the Ezrahite** is of the tribe of Levi and is likely a son of Korah. He is also the author of Psalm 88.

- **Ethan the Ezrahite** wrote Psalm 89. First Chronicles 15:19 mentions that Ethan was a singer and musician, and he was also a member of the tribe of Levi. In I Kings 4:31, Ethan is also mentioned in relation to wisdom, so it is fair to assume he was a famous wise man.

- **Moses** wrote Psalm 90. This is understood to be the oldest psalm, as Moses lived long before the rest of the known authors.

- Around forty-seven of the psalms remain anonymous. They could have all been authored by one anonymous person, but it is more likely many contributors, scribes, and holy people penned these psalms over the years.

Date: The book of Psalms was written over a span of almost 1,000 years. Because of this expansive period of time, readers can identify with the various moods and faith journeys of both the authors and the people of Israel. However, the majority of the psalms were composed during the time of David and Solomon—as is reflected in the psalms attributed to David. Many psalms were composed during the Babylonian captivity, and other psalms were composed after the Babylonian captivity had ended, around 537 BC.

What are the psalms about? The psalms contain many songs and poems, with the majority of them originally written to music and meant to be sung. These psalms would be sung in synagogues as well as outside the church. Their content ranges in theme and covers a breadth of emotions, examples of prayer, and ways to relate to God. The book of Psalms can be categorized into several themes, including lament psalms, confessional psalms, praise psalms, and instructional or didactic psalms. By including praises to God and the authors' questioning of his ways at times, the psalms show us how to have a fully authentic relationship with God.

Why are the psalms important? Both Luke and Paul, who were writers of New Testament books, believed that the book of Psalms was a source of instruction and strength. (Paul actually mentions the Psalms thirty-one times in the books attributed to him.) Since the time of the early church, psalms have been used in worship and preaching. They help provide Christians today with encouragement, comfort, and stability in every season of life.

Second Timothy 3:16 says, "All scripture is given by inspiration of God, and is profitable for doctrine, for reproof, for correction, for instruction in righteousness." No matter what we are facing, there is a psalm that we can relate to and draw hope from. Every verse and chapter of Psalms is inspired by God and is meant to draw you closer to him. Dive into the book of Psalms and experience the beauty within.

TO THE MOST HIGH AND MIGHTY PRINCE

JAMES

BY THE GRACE OF GOD
KING OF GREAT BRITAIN, FRANCE, AND
IRELAND, DEFENDER OF THE FAITH, &C.
The Translators of the Bible wish Grace, Mercy, and
Peace through JESUS CHRIST our Lord

Great and manifold were the blessings, most dread Sovereign, which Almighty God, the Father of all mercies, bestowed upon us the people of England, when first he sent Your Majesty's Royal Person to rule and reign over us. For whereas it was the expectation of many, who wished not well unto our Sion, that upon the setting of that bright Occidental Star, Queen Elizabeth of most happy memory, some thick and palpable clouds of darkness would so have overshadowed this Land, that men should have been in doubt which way they were to walk; and that it should hardly be known, who was to direct the unsettled State; the appearance of Your Majesty, as of the Sun in his strength, instantly dispelled those supposed and surmised mists, and gave unto all that were well affected exceeding cause of comfort; especially when we beheld the Government established in Your Highness, and Your hopeful Seed, by an undoubted Title, and this also accompanied with peace and tranquillity at home and abroad.

But among all our joys, there was no one that more filled our hearts than the blessed continuance of the preaching of God's sacred Word among us; which is that inestimable treasure, which excelleth all the riches of the earth;

because the fruit thereof extendeth itself, not only to the time spent in this transitory world, but directeth and disposeth men unto that eternal happiness which is above in heaven.

Then not to suffer this to fall to the ground, but rather to take it up, and to continue it in that state, wherein the famous Predecessor of Your Highness did leave it: nay, to go forward with the confidence and resolution of a Man in maintaining the truth of Christ, and propagating it far and near, is that which hath so bound and firmly knit the hearts of all Your Majesty's loyal and religious people unto You, that Your very name is precious among them: their eye doth behold You with comfort, and they bless You in their hearts, as that sanctified Person, who, under God, is the immediate Author of their true happiness. And this their contentment doth not diminish or decay, but every day increaseth and taketh strength, when they observe, that the zeal of Your Majesty toward the house of God doth not slack or go backward, but is more and more kindled, manifesting itself abroad in the farthest parts of Christendom, by writing in defence of the Truth, (which hath given such a blow unto that man of sin, as will not be healed,) and every day at home, by religious and learned discourse, by frequenting the house of God, by hearing the Word preached, by cherishing the Teachers thereof, by caring for the Church, as a most tender and loving nursing Father.

There are infinite arguments of this right Christian and religious affection in Your Majesty; but none is more forcible to declare it to others than the vehement and perpetuated desire of accomplishing and publishing of this work, which now with all humility we present unto Your Majesty. For when Your Highness has once out of deep judgment apprehended how convenient it was, that out of the Original Sacred Tongues, together with comparing of the labours, both in our own, and other foreign Languages, of many worthy men who went before us, there should be one more exact Translation of the holy Scriptures into the English Tongue; Your Majesty did never desist to urge and to excite those to whom it was commended, that the work might be hastened, and that the business might be expedited in so decent a manner, as a matter of such importance might justly require.

And now at last, by the mercy of God, and the continuance of our labours, it being brought unto such a conclusion, as that we have great hopes that the Church of England shall reap good fruit thereby; we hold it our duty to offer it to Your Majesty, not only as to our King and Sovereign, but as to the principal Mover and Author of the work: humbly craving of Your most Sacred Majesty, that since things of this quality have ever been subject to the censures of illmeaning and discontented persons, it may receive approbation and patronage from so learned and judicious a Prince as Your Highness is, whose allowance and acceptance of our labours shall more honour and encourage us than all the calumniations and hard interpretations of other men shall dismay us. So that if, on the one side, we shall be traduced by Popish Persons at home or abroad, who therefore will malign us, because we are poor instruments to make God's holy Truth to be yet more and more known unto the people, whom they desire still to keep in ignorance and darkness; or if, on the other side, we shall be maligned by selfconceited Brethren, who run their own ways, and give liking unto nothing, but what is framed by themselves, and hammered on their anvil; we may rest secure, supported within by the truth and innocency of a good conscience, having walked the ways of simplicity and integrity, as before the Lord; and sustained without by the powerful protection of Your Majesty's grace and favour, which will ever give countenance to honest and Christian endeavors against bitter censures and uncharitable imputations.

The Lord of heaven and earth bless Your Majesty with many and happy days, that, as his heavenly hand hath enriched Your Highness with many singular and extraordinary graces, so You may be the wonder of the world in this latter age for happiness and true felicity, to the honour of that great GOD, and the good of his Church, through Jesus Christ our Lord and only Saviour.

A SANCTUARY IN THE
PSALMS

BOOK 1

Psalm 1

1 Blessed *is* the man that walketh not in the
counsel of the ungodly, nor standeth in the way
of sinners, nor sitteth in the seat of the scornful.
2 But his delight *is* in the law of the LORD; and in
his law doth he meditate day and night.
3 And he shall be like a tree planted by the rivers
of water, that bringeth forth his fruit in his sea-
son; his leaf also shall not wither; and whatsoever
he doeth shall prosper.
4 The ungodly *are* not so: but *are* like the chaff
which the wind driveth away.
5 Therefore the ungodly shall not stand in the
judgment, nor sinners in the congregation of the
righteous.
6 For the LORD knoweth the way of the righ-
teous: but the way of the ungodly shall perish.

Psalm 2

1 Why do the heathen rage, and the people imag-
ine a vain thing?
2 The kings of the earth set themselves, and the
rulers take counsel together, against the LORD,
and against his anointed, *saying*,
3 Let us break their bands asunder, and cast away
their cords from us.
4 He that sitteth in the heavens shall laugh: the
Lord shall have them in derision.
5 Then shall he speak unto them in his wrath, and
vex them in his sore displeasure.
6 Yet have I set my king upon my holy hill of Zion.
7 I will declare the decree: the LORD hath said
unto me, Thou *art* my Son; this day have I begot-
ten thee.
8 Ask of me, and I shall give *thee* the heathen *for*
thine inheritance, and the uttermost parts of the
earth *for* thy possession.
9 Thou shalt break them with a rod of iron; thou
shalt dash them in pieces like a potter's vessel.
10 Be wise now therefore, O ye kings: be instruct-
ed, ye judges of the earth.
11 Serve the LORD with fear, and rejoice with
trembling.
12 Kiss the Son, lest he be angry, and ye perish
from the way, when his wrath is kindled but a lit-
tle. Blessed *are* all they that put their trust in him.

Psalm 3

A Psalm of David, when he fled from Absalom his son.

1 LORD, how are they increased that trouble me!
many *are* they that rise up against me.
2 Many *there be* which say of my soul, *There is* no
help for him in God. Selah.
3 But thou, O LORD, *art* a shield for me; my glory,
and the lifter up of mine head.
4 I cried unto the LORD with my voice, and he
heard me out of his holy hill. Selah.
5 I laid me down and slept; I awaked; for the LORD
sustained me.
6 I will not be afraid of ten thousands of people,
that have set *themselves* against me round about.
7 Arise, O LORD; save me, O my God: for thou
hast smitten all mine enemies *upon* the cheek
bone; thou hast broken the teeth of the ungodly.
8 Salvation *belongeth* unto the LORD: thy bless-
ing *is* upon thy people. Selah.

Psalm 4

To the chief Musician on Neginoth, A Psalm of David.

1 Hear me when I call, O God of my righteous-
ness: thou hast enlarged me *when I was* in distress;
have mercy upon me, and hear my prayer.
2 O ye sons of men, how long *will ye turn* my glory
into shame? how long will ye love vanity, *and* seek
after leasing? Selah.

REST JOY GRACE RENEWAL

3 But know that the LORD hath set apart him that
is godly for himself: the LORD will hear when I call
unto him.
4 Stand in awe, and sin not: commune with your
own heart upon your bed, and be still. Selah.
5 Offer the sacrifices of righteousness, and put
your trust in the LORD.
6 *There be* many that say, Who will shew us *any*
good? LORD, lift thou up the light of thy counte-
nance upon us.
7 Thou hast put gladness in my heart, more than
in the time *that* their corn and their wine
increased.
8 I will both lay me down in peace, and sleep: for
thou, LORD, only makest me dwell in safety.

Psalm 5

To the chief Musician upon Nehiloth,
A Psalm of David.

1 Give ear to my words, O LORD, consider my
meditation.
2 Hearken unto the voice of my cry, my King, and
my God: for unto thee will I pray.
3 My voice shalt thou hear in the morning, O
LORD; in the morning will I direct *my prayer* unto
thee, and will look up.
4 For thou *art* not a God that hath pleasure in
wickedness: neither shall evil dwell with thee.

5 The foolish shall not stand in thy sight: thou
hatest all workers of iniquity.
6 Thou shalt destroy them that speak leasing: the
LORD will abhor the bloody and deceitful man.
7 But as for me, I will come *into* thy house in the
multitude of thy mercy: *and* in thy fear will I wor-
ship toward thy holy temple.
8 Lead me, O LORD, in thy righteousness because
of mine enemies; make thy way straight before my
face.
9 For *there is* no faithfulness in their mouth; their
inward part *is* very wickedness; their throat *is* an
open sepulchre; they flatter with their tongue.
10 Destroy thou them, O God; let them fall by their
own counsels; cast them out in the multitude of their
transgressions; for they have rebelled against thee.
11 But let all those that put their trust in thee
rejoice: let them ever shout for joy, because thou
defendest them: let them also that love thy name
be joyful in thee.
12 For thou, LORD, wilt bless the righteous; with
favour wilt thou compass him as *with* a shield.

Psalm 6

To the chief Musician on Neginoth
upon Sheminith, A Psalm of David.

1 O LORD, rebuke me not in thine anger, neither
chasten me in thy hot displeasure.

2 Have mercy upon me, O LORD; for I *am* weak:
O LORD, heal me; for my bones are vexed.
3 My soul is also sore vexed: but thou, O LORD,
how long?
4 Return, O LORD, deliver my soul: oh save me
for thy mercies' sake.
5 For in death *there is* no remembrance of thee:
in the grave who shall give thee thanks?
6 I am weary with my groaning; all the night make
I my bed to swim; I water my couch with my tears.
7 Mine eye is consumed because of grief; it wax-
eth old because of all mine enemies.
8 Depart from me, all ye workers of iniquity; for
the LORD hath heard the voice of my weeping.
9 The LORD hath heard my supplication; the LORD
will receive my prayer.
10 Let all mine enemies be ashamed and sore
vexed: let them return *and* be ashamed suddenly.

Psalm 7

Shiggaion of David, which he sang unto the LORD, concerning the words of Cush the Benjamite.

1 O LORD my God, in thee do I put my trust: save
me from all them that persecute me, and deliver me:
2 Lest he tear my soul like a lion, rending *it* in
pieces, while *there is* none to deliver.
3 O LORD my God, If I have done this; if there be
iniquity in my hands;

PEACE COMFORT HOPE STRENGTH GRATITUDE

4 If I have rewarded evil unto him that was at
peace with me; (yea, I have delivered him that
without cause is mine enemy:)
5 Let the enemy persecute my soul, and take *it;*
yea, let him tread down my life upon the earth,
and lay mine honour in the dust. Selah.
6 Arise, O LORD, in thine anger, lift up thyself
because of the rage of mine enemies: and awake
for me *to* the judgment *that* thou hast command-
ed.
7 So shall the congregation of the people com-
pass thee about: for their sakes therefore return
thou on high.
8 The LORD shall judge the people: judge me, O
LORD, according to my righteousness, and accord-
ing to mine integrity *that is* in me.
9 Oh let the wickedness of the wicked come to
an end; but establish the just: for the righteous
God trieth the hearts and reins.
10 My defence *is* of God, which saveth the
upright in heart.
11 God judgeth the righteous, and God is angry
with the wicked every day.
12 If he turn not, he will whet his sword; he hath
bent his bow, and made it ready.
13 He hath also prepared for him the instruments
of death; he ordaineth his arrows against the per-
secutors.

14 Behold, he travaileth with iniquity, and hath
conceived mischief, and brought forth falsehood.
15 He made a pit, and digged it, and is fallen into
the ditch *which* he made.
16 His mischief shall return upon his own head,
and his violent dealing shall come down upon his
own pate.
17 I will praise the LORD according to his righ-
teousness: and will sing praise to the name of the
LORD most high.

Psalm 8

To the chief Musician upon Gittith,
A Psalm of David.

1 O LORD, our Lord, how excellent *is* thy name in
all the earth! who hast set thy glory above the
heavens.
2 Out of the mouth of babes and sucklings hast thou
ordained strength because of thine enemies, that
thou mightest still the enemy and the avenger.
3 When I consider thy heavens, the work of thy
fingers, the moon and the stars, which thou hast
ordained;
4 What is man, that thou art mindful of him? and
the son of man, that thou visitest him?
5 For thou hast made him a little lower than the
angels, and hast crowned him with glory and hon-
our.

6 Thou madest him to have dominion over the
works of thy hands; thou hast put all *things* under
his feet:
7 All sheep and oxen, yea, and the beasts of the
field;
8 The fowl of the air, and the fish of the sea, *and*
whatsoever passeth through the paths of the
seas.
9 O LORD our Lord, how excellent *is* thy name in
all the earth!

Psalm 9

To the chief Musician upon Muth-labben,
A Psalm of David.

1 I will praise *thee*, O LORD, with my whole heart;
I will shew forth all thy marvellous works.
2 I will be glad and rejoice in thee: I will sing praise
to thy name, O thou most High.
3 When mine enemies are turned back, they shall
fall and perish at thy presence.
4 For thou hast maintained my right and my
cause; thou satest in the throne judging right.
5 Thou hast rebuked the heathen, thou hast
destroyed the wicked, thou hast put out their
name for ever and ever.
6 O thou enemy, destructions are come to a per-
petual end: and thou hast destroyed cities; their
memorial is perished with them.

REST JOY GRACE RENEWAL

7 But the LORD shall endure for ever: he hath pre-
pared his throne for judgment.
8 And he shall judge the world in righteousness,
he shall minister judgment to the people in
uprightness.
9 The LORD also will be a refuge for the oppressed,
a refuge in times of trouble.
10 And they that know thy name will put their
trust in thee: for thou, LORD, hast not forsaken
them that seek thee.
11 Sing praises to the LORD, which dwelleth in
Zion: declare among the people his doings.
12 When he maketh inquisition for blood, he
remembereth them: he forgetteth not the cry of
the humble.
13 Have mercy upon me, O LORD; consider my
trouble *which I suffer* of them that hate me, thou
that liftest me up from the gates of death:
14 That I may shew forth all thy praise in the gates
of the daughter of Zion: I will rejoice in thy salva-
tion.
15 The heathen are sunk down in the pit *that* they
made: in the net which they hid is their own foot
taken.
16 The LORD is known *by* the judgment *which* he
executeth: the wicked is snared in the work of his
own hands. Higgaion. Selah.

17 The wicked shall be turned into hell, *and* all the
nations that forget God.
18 For the needy shall not alway be forgotten:
the expectation of the poor shall *not* perish for
ever.
19 Arise, O LORD; let not man prevail: let the hea-
then be judged in thy sight.
20 Put them in fear, O LORD: *that* the nations
may know themselves *to be but* men. Selah.

Psalm 10

1 Why standest thou afar off, O LORD? *why* hidest
thou *thyself* in times of trouble?
2 The wicked in *his* pride doth persecute the poor:
let them be taken in the devices that they have
imagined.
3 For the wicked boasteth of his heart's desire,
and blesseth the covetous, *whom* the LORD abhor-
reth.
4 The wicked, through the pride of his counte-
nance, will not seek *after God:* God *is* not in all his
thoughts.
5 His ways are always grievous; thy judgments *are*
far above out of his sight: *as for* all his enemies, he
puffeth at them.
6 He hath said in his heart, I shall not be moved:
for *I shall* never *be* in adversity.

7 His mouth is full of cursing and deceit and
fraud: under his tongue *is* mischief and vanity.
8 He sitteth in the lurking places of the villages:
in the secret places doth he murder the innocent:
his eyes are privily set against the poor.
9 He lieth in wait secretly as a lion in his den: he
lieth in wait to catch the poor: he doth catch the
poor, when he draweth him into his net.
10 He croucheth, *and* humbleth himself, that the
poor may fall by his strong ones.
11 He hath said in his heart, God hath forgotten:
he hideth his face; he will never see *it.*
12 Arise, O LORD; O God, lift up thine hand: for-
get not the humble.
13 Wherefore doth the wicked contemn God?
he hath said in his heart, Thou wilt not require *it.*
14 Thou hast seen *it;* for thou beholdest mischief
and spite, to requite *it* with thy hand: the poor
committeth himself unto thee; thou art the help-
er of the fatherless.
15 Break thou the arm of the wicked and the
evil *man:* seek out his wickedness *till* thou find
none.
16 The LORD *is* King for ever and ever: the hea-
then are perished out of his land.
17 LORD, thou hast heard the desire of the hum-
ble: thou wilt prepare their heart, thou wilt cause
thine ear to hear:

PEACE COMFORT HOPE STRENGTH GRATITUDE

18 To judge the fatherless and the oppressed, that
the man of the earth may no more oppress.

Psalm 11

To the chief Musician, A Psalm *of David.*

1 In the LORD put I my trust: how say ye to my
soul, Flee *as* a bird to your mountain?
2 For, lo, the wicked bend *their* bow, they make
ready their arrow upon the string, that they may
privily shoot at the upright in heart.
3 If the foundations be destroyed, what can the
righteous do?
4 The LORD *is* in his holy temple, the LORD's
throne *is* in heaven: his eyes behold, his eyelids
try, the children of men.
5 The LORD trieth the righteous: but the wicked
and him that loveth violence his soul hateth.
6 Upon the wicked he shall rain snares, fire and
brimstone, and an horrible tempest: *this shall be*
the portion of their cup.
7 For the righteous LORD loveth righteousness;
his countenance doth behold the upright.

Psalm 12

To the chief Musician upon Sheminith,
A Psalm of David.

1 Help, LORD; for the godly man ceaseth; for the
faithful fail from among the children of men.

2 They speak vanity every one with his neighbour:
with flattering lips *and* with a double heart do they
speak.
3 The LORD shall cut off all flattering lips, *and* the
tongue that speaketh proud things:
4 Who have said, With our tongue will we prevail;
our lips *are* our own: who *is* lord over us?
5 For the oppression of the poor, for the sighing
of the needy, now will I arise, saith the LORD; I will
set *him* in safety *from him that* puffeth at him.
6 The words of the LORD *are* pure words: *as* silver
tried in a furnace of earth, purified seven times.
7 Thou shalt keep them, O LORD, thou shalt pre-
serve them from this generation for ever.
8 The wicked walk on every side, when the vilest
men are exalted.

Psalm 13

To the chief Musician, A Psalm of David.

1 How long wilt thou forget me, O LORD? for
ever? how long wilt thou hide thy face from me?
2 How long shall I take counsel in my soul, *having*
sorrow in my heart daily? how long shall mine
enemy be exalted over me?
3 Consider *and* hear me, O LORD my God: light-
en mine eyes, lest I sleep the *sleep of* death;
4 Lest mine enemy say, I have prevailed against him;
and those that trouble me rejoice when I am moved.

5 But I have trusted in thy mercy; my heart shall
rejoice in thy salvation.
6 I will sing unto the LORD, because he hath dealt
bountifully with me.

Psalm 14

To the chief Musician,
A Psalm *of David.*

1 The fool hath said in his heart, *There is* no God.
They are corrupt, they have done abominable
works, *there is* none that doeth good.
2 The LORD looked down from heaven upon the
children of men, to see if there were any that did
understand, *and* seek God.
3 They are all gone aside, they are *all* together
become filthy: *there is* none that doeth good, no,
not one.
4 Have all the workers of iniquity no knowledge?
who eat up my people *as* they eat bread, and call
not upon the LORD.
5 There were they in great fear: for God *is* in the
generation of the righteous.
6 Ye have shamed the counsel of the poor,
because the LORD *is* his refuge.
7 Oh that the salvation of Israel *were come* out of
Zion! when the LORD bringeth back the captivity
of his people, Jacob shall rejoice, *and* Israel shall
be glad.

REST JOY GRACE RENEWAL

Psalm 15

A Psalm of David.

1 LORD, who shall abide in thy tabernacle? who
shall dwell in thy holy hill?
2 He that walketh uprightly, and worketh righ-
teousness, and speaketh the truth in his heart.
3 *He that* backbiteth not with his tongue, nor
doeth evil to his neighbour, nor taketh up a
reproach against his neighbour.
4 In whose eyes a vile person is contemned; but
he honoureth them that fear the LORD. *He that*
sweareth to *his own* hurt, and changeth not.
5 *He that* putteth not out his money to usury, nor
taketh reward against the innocent. He that doeth
these *things* shall never be moved.

Psalm 16

Michtam of David.

1 Preserve me, O God: for in thee do I put my trust.
2 *O my soul*, thou hast said unto the LORD, Thou
art my Lord: my goodness *extendeth* not to thee;
3 *But* to the saints that *are* in the earth, and *to* the
excellent, in whom *is* all my delight.
4 Their sorrows shall be multiplied *that* hasten *after*
another *god:* their drink offerings of blood will I not
offer, nor take up their names into my lips.
5 The LORD *is* the portion of mine inheritance and
of my cup: thou maintainest my lot.

6 The lines are fallen unto me in pleasant *places;*
yea, I have a goodly heritage.
7 I will bless the LORD, who hath given me coun-
sel: my reins also instruct me in the night sea-
sons.
8 I have set the LORD always before me: because
he is at my right hand, I shall not be moved.
9 Therefore my heart is glad, and my glory rejoiceth:
my flesh also shall rest in hope.
10 For thou wilt not leave my soul in hell; nei-
ther wilt thou suffer thine Holy One to see cor-
ruption.
11 Thou wilt shew me the path of life: in thy pres-
ence *is* fulness of joy; at thy right hand *there are*
pleasures for evermore.

Psalm 17

A Prayer of David.

1 Hear the right, O LORD, attend unto my cry,
give ear unto my prayer, *that goeth* not out of
feigned lips.
2 Let my sentence come forth from thy pres-
ence; let thine eyes behold the things that are
equal.
3 Thou hast proved mine heart; thou hast visited
me in the night; thou hast tried me, *and* shalt find
nothing; I am purposed *that* my mouth shall not
transgress.

REST JOY GRACE RENEWAL

4 Concerning the works of men, by the word of
thy lips I have kept *me from* the paths of the
destroyer.
5 Hold up my goings in thy paths, *that* my foot-
steps slip not.
6 I have called upon thee, for thou wilt hear me,
O God: incline thine ear unto me, *and hear* my
speech.
7 Shew thy marvellous lovingkindness, O thou
that savest by thy right hand them which put
their trust *in thee* from those that rise up *against
them.*
8 Keep me as the apple of the eye, hide me under
the shadow of thy wings,
9 From the wicked that oppress me, *from* my
deadly enemies, *who* compass me about.
10 They are inclosed in their own fat: with their
mouth they speak proudly.
11 They have now compassed us in our steps: they
have set their eyes bowing down to the earth;
12 Like as a lion *that* is greedy of his prey, and as
it were a young lion lurking in secret places.
13 Arise, O LORD, disappoint him, cast him down:
deliver my soul from the wicked, *which is* thy
sword:
14 From men *which are* thy hand, O LORD, from
men of the world, *which have* their portion in *this*
life, and whose belly thou fillest with thy hid

treasure: they are full of children, and leave the
rest of their *substance* to their babes.
15 As for me, I will behold thy face in righteousness:
I shall be satisfied, when I awake, with thy likeness.

Psalm 18

To the chief Musician, A Psalm *of David, the servant of the* LORD, *who spake unto the* LORD *the words of this song in the day* that *the* LORD *delivered him from the hand of all his enemies, and from the hand of Saul: And he said,*

1 I will love thee, O LORD, my strength.
2 The LORD *is* my rock, and my fortress, and my
deliverer; my God, my strength, in whom I will
trust; my buckler, and the horn of my salvation,
and my high tower.
3 I will call upon the LORD, *who is worthy* to be
praised: so shall I be saved from mine enemies.
4 The sorrows of death compassed me, and the
floods of ungodly men made me afraid.
5 The sorrows of hell compassed me about: the
snares of death prevented me.
6 In my distress I called upon the LORD, and cried
unto my God: he heard my voice out of his temple,
and my cry came before him, *even* into his ears.
7 Then the earth shook and trembled; the foun-
dations also of the hills moved and were shaken,
because he was wroth.

8 There went up a smoke out of his nostrils, and
fire out of his mouth devoured: coals were kindled
by it.
9 He bowed the heavens also, and came down:
and darkness *was* under his feet.
10 And he rode upon a cherub, and did fly: yea,
he did fly upon the wings of the wind.
11 He made darkness his secret place; his pavilion
round about him *were* dark waters *and* thick clouds
of the skies.
12 At the brightness *that was* before him his thick
clouds passed, hail *stones* and coals of fire.
13 The LORD also thundered in the heavens, and the
Highest gave his voice; hail *stones* and coals of fire.
14 Yea, he sent out his arrows, and scattered
them; and he shot out lightnings, and discomfit-
ed them.
15 Then the channels of waters were seen, and the
foundations of the world were discovered at thy
rebuke, O LORD, at the blast of the breath of thy
nostrils.
16 He sent from above, he took me, he drew me
out of many waters.
17 He delivered me from my strong enemy, and
from them which hated me: for they were too
strong for me.
18 They prevented me in the day of my calamity:
but the LORD was my stay.

19 He brought me forth also into a large place; he
delivered me, because he delighted in me.
20 The LORD rewarded me according to my righ-
teousness; according to the cleanness of my
hands hath he recompensed me.
21 For I have kept the ways of the LORD, and have
not wickedly departed from my God.
22 For all his judgments *were* before me, and I did
not put away his statutes from me.
23 I was also upright before him, and I kept myself
from mine iniquity.
24 Therefore hath the LORD recompensed me
according to my righteousness, according to the
cleanness of my hands in his eyesight.
25 With the merciful thou wilt shew thyself mer-
ciful; with an upright man thou wilt shew thyself
upright;
26 With the pure thou wilt shew thyself pure; and
with the froward thou wilt shew thyself froward.
27 For thou wilt save the afflicted people; but wilt
bring down high looks.
28 For thou wilt light my candle: the LORD my
God will enlighten my darkness.
29 For by thee I have run through a troop; and by
my God have I leaped over a wall.
30 *As for* God, his way *is* perfect: the word of the
LORD is tried: he *is* a buckler to all those that trust
in him.

31 For who *is* God save the LORD? or who *is* a rock
save our God?
32 *It is* God that girdeth me with strength, and
maketh my way perfect.
33 He maketh my feet like hinds' *feet*, and setteth
me upon my high places.
34 He teacheth my hands to war, so that a bow
of steel is broken by mine arms.
35 Thou hast also given me the shield of thy sal-
vation: and thy right hand hath holden me up, and
thy gentleness hath made me great.
36 Thou hast enlarged my steps under me, that
my feet did not slip.
37 I have pursued mine enemies, and overtaken
them: neither did I turn again till they were con-
sumed.
38 I have wounded them that they were not able
to rise: they are fallen under my feet.
39 For thou hast girded me with strength unto
the battle: thou hast subdued under me those that
rose up against me.
40 Thou hast also given me the necks of mine
enemies; that I might destroy them that hate me.
41 They cried, but *there was* none to save *them*:
even unto the LORD, but he answered them not.
42 Then did I beat them small as the dust before
the wind: I did cast them out as the dirt in the
streets.

43 Thou hast delivered me from the strivings of
the people; *and* thou hast made me the head of
the heathen: a people *whom* I have not known shall
serve me.
44 As soon as they hear of me, they shall obey
me: the strangers shall submit themselves unto
me.
45 The strangers shall fade away, and be afraid out
of their close places.
46 The LORD liveth; and blessed *be* my rock; and
let the God of my salvation be exalted.
47 *It is* God that avengeth me, and subdueth the
people under me.
48 He delivereth me from mine enemies: yea,
thou liftest me up above those that rise up against
me: thou hast delivered me from the violent
man.
49 Therefore will I give thanks unto thee, O LORD,
among the heathen, and sing praises unto thy
name.
50 Great deliverance giveth he to his king; and
sheweth mercy to his anointed, to David, and to
his seed for evermore.

Psalm 19

To the chief Musician, A Psalm of David.

1 The heavens declare the glory of God; and the
firmament sheweth his handywork.

REST JOY GRACE RENEWAL

2 Day unto day uttereth speech, and night unto
night sheweth knowledge.
3 *There is* no speech nor language, *where* their
voice is not heard.
4 Their line is gone out through all the earth, and
their words to the end of the world. In them hath
he set a tabernacle for the sun,
5 Which *is* as a bridegroom coming out of his cham-
ber, *and* rejoiceth as a strong man to run a race.
6 His going forth *is* from the end of the heaven,
and his circuit unto the ends of it: and there is
nothing hid from the heat thereof.
7 The law of the LORD *is* perfect, converting the
soul: the testimony of the LORD *is* sure, making
wise the simple.
8 The statutes of the LORD *are* right, rejoicing the
heart: the commandment of the LORD *is* pure,
enlightening the eyes.
9 The fear of the LORD *is* clean, enduring for ever:
the judgments of the LORD *are* true *and* righteous
altogether.
10 More to be desired *are they* than gold, yea,
than much fine gold: sweeter also than honey and
the honeycomb.
11 Moreover by them is thy servant warned: *and*
in keeping of them *there is* great reward.
12 Who can understand *his* errors? cleanse thou
me from secret *faults*.

13 Keep back thy servant also from presumptu-
ous *sins;* let them not have dominion over me:
then shall I be upright, and I shall be innocent
from the great transgression.
14 Let the words of my mouth, and the meditation
of my heart, be acceptable in thy sight, O LORD,
my strength, and my redeemer.

Psalm 20

To the chief Musician,
A Psalm of David.

1 The LORD hear thee in the day of trouble; the
name of the God of Jacob defend thee;
2 Send thee help from the sanctuary, and
strengthen thee out of Zion;
3 Remember all thy offerings, and accept thy
burnt sacrifice; Selah.
4 Grant thee according to thine own heart, and
fulfil all thy counsel.
5 We will rejoice in thy salvation, and in the name
of our God we will set up *our* banners: the LORD
fulfil all thy petitions.
6 Now know I that the LORD saveth his anointed;
he will hear him from his holy heaven with the sav-
ing strength of his right hand.
7 Some *trust* in chariots, and some in horses: but
we will remember the name of the LORD our
God.

8 They are brought down and fallen: but we are
risen, and stand upright.
9 Save, LORD: let the king hear us when we call.

Psalm 21

To the chief Musician, A Psalm of David.

1 The king shall joy in thy strength, O LORD; and
in thy salvation how greatly shall he rejoice!
2 Thou hast given him his heart's desire, and hast
not withholden the request of his lips. Selah.
3 For thou preventest him with the blessings of
goodness: thou settest a crown of pure gold on his
head.
4 He asked life of thee, *and* thou gavest *it* him,
even length of days for ever and ever.
5 His glory *is* great in thy salvation: honour and
majesty hast thou laid upon him.
6 For thou hast made him most blessed for ever:
thou hast made him exceeding glad with thy
countenance.
7 For the king trusteth in the LORD, and through
the mercy of the most High he shall not be
moved.
8 Thine hand shall find out all thine enemies: thy
right hand shall find out those that hate thee.
9 Thou shalt make them as a fiery oven in the
time of thine anger: the LORD shall swallow them
up in his wrath, and the fire shall devour them.

10 Their fruit shalt thou destroy from the earth,
and their seed from among the children of men.
11 For they intended evil against thee: they imag-
ined a mischievous device, *which* they are not able
to perform.
12 Therefore shalt thou make them turn their
back, *when* thou shalt make ready *thine arrows*
upon thy strings against the face of them.
13 Be thou exalted, LORD, in thine own strength:
so will we sing and praise thy power.

Psalm 22

To the chief Musician upon Aijeleth Shahar,
A Psalm of David.

1 My God, my God, why hast thou forsaken me?
why art thou so far from helping me, *and from* the
words of my roaring?
2 O my God, I cry in the daytime, but thou hear-
est not; and in the night season, and am not
silent.
3 But thou *art* holy, *O thou* that inhabitest the
praises of Israel.
4 Our fathers trusted in thee: they trusted, and
thou didst deliver them.
5 They cried unto thee, and were delivered: they
trusted in thee, and were not confounded.
6 But I *am* a worm, and no man; a reproach of
men, and despised of the people.

REST JOY GRACE RENEWAL

7 All they that see me laugh me to scorn: they
shoot out the lip, they shake the head, *saying*,
8 He trusted on the LORD *that* he would deliver
him: let him deliver him, seeing he delighted in him.
9 But thou *art* he that took me out of the womb:
thou didst make me hope *when I was* upon my
mother's breasts.
10 I was cast upon thee from the womb: thou *art*
my God from my mother's belly.
11 Be not far from me; for trouble *is* near; for *there*
is none to help.
12 Many bulls have compassed me: strong *bulls* of
Bashan have beset me round.
13 They gaped upon me *with* their mouths, *as* a
ravening and a roaring lion.
14 I am poured out like water, and all my bones
are out of joint: my heart is like wax; it is melted
in the midst of my bowels.
15 My strength is dried up like a potsherd; and my
tongue cleaveth to my jaws; and thou hast brought
me into the dust of death.
16 For dogs have compassed me: the assembly of
the wicked have inclosed me: they pierced my
hands and my feet.
17 I may tell all my bones: they look *and* stare
upon me.
18 They part my garments among them, and cast
lots upon my vesture.

19 But be not thou far from me, O LORD: O my
strength, haste thee to help me.
20 Deliver my soul from the sword; my darling
from the power of the dog.
21 Save me from the lion's mouth: for thou hast
heard me from the horns of the unicorns.
22 I will declare thy name unto my brethren: in
the midst of the congregation will I praise thee.
23 Ye that fear the LORD, praise him; all ye the seed
of Jacob, glorify him; and fear him, all ye the seed
of Israel.
24 For he hath not despised nor abhorred the afflic-
tion of the afflicted; neither hath he hid his face
from him; but when he cried unto him, he heard.
25 My praise *shall be* of thee in the great congre-
gation: I will pay my vows before them that fear him.
26 The meek shall eat and be satisfied: they shall
praise the LORD that seek him: your heart shall live
for ever.
27 All the ends of the world shall remember and
turn unto the LORD: and all the kindreds of the
nations shall worship before thee.
28 For the kingdom *is* the LORD'S: and he *is* the
governor among the nations.
29 All *they that be* fat upon earth shall eat and
worship: all they that go down to the dust shall
bow before him: and none can keep alive his own
soul.

30 A seed shall serve him; it shall be accounted
to the Lord for a generation.
31 They shall come, and shall declare his righteous-
ness unto a people that shall be born, that he hath
done *this.*

Psalm 23

A Psalm of David.

1 The LORD *is* my shepherd; I shall not want.
2 He maketh me to lie down in green pastures:
he leadeth me beside the still waters.
3 He restoreth my soul: he leadeth me in the
paths of righteousness for his name's sake.
4 Yea, though I walk through the valley of the shad-
ow of death, I will fear no evil: for thou *art* with me;
thy rod and thy staff they comfort me.
5 Thou preparest a table before me in the pres-
ence of mine enemies: thou anointest my head
with oil; my cup runneth over.
6 Surely goodness and mercy shall follow me all
the days of my life: and I will dwell in the house of
the LORD for ever.

Psalm 24

A Psalm of David.

1 The earth *is* the LORD'S, and the fulness there-
of; the world, and they that dwell therein.

2 For he hath founded it upon the seas, and
established it upon the floods.
3 Who shall ascend into the hill of the LORD? or
who shall stand in his holy place?
4 He that hath clean hands, and a pure heart; who
hath not lifted up his soul unto vanity, nor sworn
deceitfully.
5 He shall receive the blessing from the LORD,
and righteousness from the God of his salvation.
6 This *is* the generation of them that seek him,
that seek thy face, O Jacob. Selah.
7 Lift up your heads, O ye gates; and be ye lift up,
ye everlasting doors; and the King of glory shall
come in.
8 Who *is* this King of glory? The LORD strong and
mighty, the LORD mighty in battle.
9 Lift up your heads, O ye gates; even lift *them*
up, ye everlasting doors; and the King of glory
shall come in.
10 Who is this King of glory? The LORD of hosts,
he *is* the King of glory. Selah.

Psalm 25

A Psalm *of David.*

1 Unto thee, O LORD, do I lift up my soul.
2 O my God, I trust in thee: let me not be
ashamed, let not mine enemies triumph over me.

3 Yea, let none that wait on thee be ashamed: let
them be ashamed which transgress without cause.
4 Shew me thy ways, O LORD; teach me thy
paths.
5 Lead me in thy truth, and teach me: for thou
art the God of my salvation; on thee do I wait all
the day.
6 Remember, O LORD, thy tender mercies and thy
lovingkindnesses; for they *have been* ever of old.
7 Remember not the sins of my youth, nor my
transgressions: according to thy mercy remem-
ber thou me for thy goodness' sake, O LORD.
8 Good and upright *is* the LORD: therefore will he
teach sinners in the way.
9 The meek will he guide in judgment: and the
meek will he teach his way.
10 All the paths of the LORD *are* mercy and truth
unto such as keep his covenant and his testimo-
nies.
11 For thy name's sake, O LORD, pardon mine
iniquity; for it *is* great.
12 What man *is* he that feareth the LORD? him
shall he teach in the way *that* he shall choose.
13 His soul shall dwell at ease; and his seed shall
inherit the earth.
14 The secret of the LORD *is* with them that fear
him; and he will shew them his covenant.

15 Mine eyes *are* ever toward the LORD; for he
shall pluck my feet out of the net.
16 Turn thee unto me, and have mercy upon me;
for I *am* desolate and afflicted.
17 The troubles of my heart are enlarged: O bring
thou me out of my distresses.
18 Look upon mine affliction and my pain; and
forgive all my sins.
19 Consider mine enemies; for they are many;
and they hate me with cruel hatred.
20 O keep my soul, and deliver me: let me not be
ashamed; for I put my trust in thee.
21 Let integrity and uprightness preserve me; for
I wait on thee.
22 Redeem Israel, O God, out of all his troubles.

Psalm 26

A Psalm *of David.*

1 Judge me, O LORD; for I have walked in mine
integrity: I have trusted also in the LORD; *there-*
fore I shall not slide.
2 Examine me, O LORD, and prove me; try my
reins and my heart.
3 For thy lovingkindness *is* before mine eyes: and
I have walked in thy truth.
4 I have not sat with vain persons, neither will I
go in with dissemblers.

REST JOY GRACE RENEWAL

5 I have hated the congregation of evildoers; and
will not sit with the wicked.
6 I will wash mine hands in innocency: so will I
compass thine altar, O LORD:
7 That I may publish with the voice of thanksgiv-
ing, and tell of all thy wondrous works.
8 LORD, I have loved the habitation of thy house,
and the place where thine honour dwelleth.
9 Gather not my soul with sinners, nor my life
with bloody men:
10 In whose hands *is* mischief, and their right hand
is full of bribes.
11 But as for me, I will walk in mine integrity:
redeem me, and be merciful unto me.
12 My foot standeth in an even place: in the con-
gregations will I bless the LORD.

Psalm 27

A Psalm *of David.*

1 The LORD *is* my light and my salvation; whom
shall I fear? the LORD *is* the strength of my life; of
whom shall I be afraid?
2 When the wicked, *even* mine enemies and my
foes, came upon me to eat up my flesh, they
stumbled and fell.
3 Though an host should encamp against me, my
heart shall not fear: though war should rise against
me, in this *will* I *be* confident.

PEACE COMFORT HOPE STRENGTH GRATITUDE

4 One *thing* have I desired of the LORD, that will
I seek after; that I may dwell in the house of the
LORD all the days of my life, to behold the beau-
ty of the LORD, and to enquire in his temple.
5 For in the time of trouble he shall hide me in his
pavilion: in the secret of his tabernacle shall he
hide me; he shall set me up upon a rock.
6 And now shall mine head be lifted up above
mine enemies round about me: therefore will I
offer in his tabernacle sacrifices of joy; I will sing,
yea, I will sing praises unto the LORD.
7 Hear, O LORD, *when* I cry with my voice: have
mercy also upon me, and answer me.
8 *When thou saidst,* Seek ye my face; my heart
said unto thee, Thy face, LORD, will I seek.
9 Hide not thy face *far* from me; put not thy ser-
vant away in anger: thou hast been my help; leave
me not, neither forsake me, O God of my salva-
tion.
10 When my father and my mother forsake me,
then the LORD will take me up.
11 Teach me thy way, O LORD, and lead me in a
plain path, because of mine enemies.
12 Deliver me not over unto the will of mine ene-
mies: for false witnesses are risen up against me,
and such as breathe out cruelty.
13 *I had fainted,* unless I had believed to see the
goodness of the LORD in the land of the living.

REST JOY GRACE RENEWAL

14 Wait on the LORD: be of good courage, and he
shall strengthen thine heart: wait, I say, on the
LORD.

Psalm 28

A Psalm *of David.*

1 Unto thee will I cry, O LORD my rock; be not
silent to me: lest, *if* thou be silent to me, I become
like them that go down into the pit.
2 Hear the voice of my supplications, when I cry
unto thee, when I lift up my hands toward thy holy
oracle.
3 Draw me not away with the wicked, and with
the workers of iniquity, which speak peace to their
neighbours, but mischief *is* in their hearts.
4 Give them according to their deeds, and
according to the wickedness of their endeavours:
give them after the work of their hands; render to
them their desert.
5 Because they regard not the works of the LORD,
nor the operation of his hands, he shall destroy
them, and not build them up.
6 Blessed *be* the LORD, because he hath heard the
voice of my supplications.
7 The LORD *is* my strength and my shield; my
heart trusted in him, and I am helped: therefore
my heart greatly rejoiceth; and with my song will
I praise him.

8 The LORD *is* their strength, and he *is* the saving
strength of his anointed.
9 Save thy people, and bless thine inheritance:
feed them also, and lift them up for ever.

Psalm 29

A Psalm of David.

1 Give unto the LORD, O ye mighty, give unto the
LORD glory and strength.
2 Give unto the LORD the glory due unto his
name; worship the LORD in the beauty of holi-
ness.
3 The voice of the LORD *is* upon the waters: the
God of glory thundereth: the LORD *is* upon many
waters.
4 The voice of the LORD *is* powerful; the voice of
the LORD *is* full of majesty.
5 The voice of the LORD breaketh the cedars; yea,
the LORD breaketh the cedars of Lebanon.
6 He maketh them also to skip like a calf; Leba-
non and Sirion like a young unicorn.
7 The voice of the LORD divideth the flames of
fire.
8 The voice of the LORD shaketh the wilderness;
the LORD shaketh the wilderness of Kadesh.
9 The voice of the LORD maketh the hinds to
calve, and discovereth the forests: and in his tem-
ple doth every one speak of *his* glory.

10 The LORD sitteth upon the flood; yea, the LORD
sitteth King for ever.
11 The LORD will give strength unto his people; the
LORD will bless his people with peace.

Psalm 30

A Psalm and *Song* at *the dedication of the house of David.*

1 I will extol thee, O LORD; for thou hast lifted
me up, and hast not made my foes to rejoice over
me.
2 O LORD my God, I cried unto thee, and thou
hast healed me.
3 O LORD, thou hast brought up my soul from the
grave: thou hast kept me alive, that I should not
go down to the pit.
4 Sing unto the LORD, O ye saints of his, and give
thanks at the remembrance of his holiness.
5 For his anger *endureth but* a moment; in his
favour is life: weeping may endure for a night, but
joy *cometh* in the morning.
6 And in my prosperity I said, I shall never be
moved.
7 LORD, by thy favour thou hast made my moun-
tain to stand strong: thou didst hide thy face, *and*
I was troubled.
8 I cried to thee, O LORD; and unto the LORD I
made supplication.

9 What profit *is there* in my blood, when I go down
to the pit? Shall the dust praise thee? shall it
declare thy truth?
10 Hear, O LORD, and have mercy upon me:
LORD, be thou my helper.
11 Thou hast turned for me my mourning into
dancing: thou hast put off my sackcloth, and gird-
ed me with gladness;
12 To the end that *my* glory may sing praise to
thee, and not be silent. O LORD my God, I will give
thanks unto thee for ever.

Psalm 31

To the chief Musician,
A Psalm of David.

1 In thee, O LORD, do I put my trust; let me never
be ashamed: deliver me in thy righteousness.
2 Bow down thine ear to me; deliver me speedi-
ly: be thou my strong rock, for an house of
defence to save me.
3 For thou *art* my rock and my fortress; there-
fore for thy name's sake lead me, and guide me.
4 Pull me out of the net that they have laid priv-
ily for me: for thou *art* my strength.
5 Into thine hand I commit my spirit: thou hast
redeemed me, O LORD God of truth.
6 I have hated them that regard lying vanities:
but I trust in the LORD.

7 I will be glad and rejoice in thy mercy: for thou
hast considered my trouble; thou hast known my
soul in adversities;
8 And hast not shut me up into the hand of the
enemy: thou hast set my feet in a large room.
9 Have mercy upon me, O LORD, for I am in trou-
ble: mine eye is consumed with grief, *yea*, my soul
and my belly.
10 For my life is spent with grief, and my years
with sighing: my strength faileth because of mine
iniquity, and my bones are consumed.
11 I was a reproach among all mine enemies, but
especially among my neighbours, and a fear to
mine acquaintance: they that did see me without
fled from me.
12 I am forgotten as a dead man out of mind: I am
like a broken vessel.
13 For I have heard the slander of many: fear
was on every side: while they took counsel
together against me, they devised to take away
my life.
14 But I trusted in thee, O LORD: I said, Thou *art*
my God.
15 My times *are* in thy hand: deliver me from the
hand of mine enemies, and from them that per-
secute me.
16 Make thy face to shine upon thy servant: save
me for thy mercies' sake.

17 Let me not be ashamed, O LORD; for I have
called upon thee: let the wicked be ashamed, *and*
let them be silent in the grave.
18 Let the lying lips be put to silence; which speak
grievous things proudly and contemptuously
against the righteous.
19 *Oh* how great *is* thy goodness, which thou hast
laid up for them that fear thee; *which* thou hast
wrought for them that trust in thee before the
sons of men!
20 Thou shalt hide them in the secret of thy pres-
ence from the pride of man: thou shalt keep them
secretly in a pavilion from the strife of tongues.
21 Blessed *be* the LORD: for he hath shewed me
his marvellous kindness in a strong city.
22 For I said in my haste, I am cut off from before
thine eyes: nevertheless thou heardest the voice
of my supplications when I cried unto thee.
23 O love the LORD, all ye his saints: *for* the LORD
preserveth the faithful, and plentifully rewardeth
the proud doer.
24 Be of good courage, and he shall strengthen
your heart, all ye that hope in the LORD.

Psalm 32

A Psalm *of David, Maschil.*

1 Blessed *is he whose* transgression *is* forgiven,
whose sin *is* covered.

2 Blessed *is* the man unto whom the LORD imput-
eth not iniquity, and in whose spirit *there is* no guile.
3 When I kept silence, my bones waxed old
through my roaring all the day long.
4 For day and night thy hand was heavy upon me:
my moisture is turned into the drought of sum-
mer. Selah.
5 I acknowledged my sin unto thee, and mine
iniquity have I not hid. I said, I will confess my
transgressions unto the LORD; and thou forgavest
the iniquity of my sin. Selah.
6 For this shall every one that is godly pray unto
thee in a time when thou mayest be found: sure-
ly in the floods of great waters they shall not come
nigh unto him.
7 Thou *art* my hiding place; thou shalt preserve
me from trouble; thou shalt compass me about
with songs of deliverance. Selah.
8 I will instruct thee and teach thee in the way
which thou shalt go: I will guide thee with mine eye.
9 Be ye not as the horse, *or* as the mule, *which* have
no understanding: whose mouth must be held in
with bit and bridle, lest they come near unto thee.
10 Many sorrows *shall be* to the wicked: but he
that trusteth in the LORD, mercy shall compass
him about.
11 Be glad in the LORD, and rejoice, ye righteous:
and shout for joy, all *ye that are* upright in heart.

Psalm 33

1 Rejoice in the LORD, O ye righteous: *for* praise
is comely for the upright.
2 Praise the LORD with harp: sing unto him with
the psaltery *and* an instrument of ten strings.
3 Sing unto him a new song; play skilfully with a
loud noise.
4 For the word of the LORD *is* right; and all his
works *are done* in truth.
5 He loveth righteousness and judgment: the
earth is full of the goodness of the LORD.
6 By the word of the LORD were the heavens
made; and all the host of them by the breath of
his mouth.
7 He gathereth the waters of the sea together as
an heap: he layeth up the depth in storehouses.
8 Let all the earth fear the LORD: let all the inhab-
itants of the world stand in awe of him.
9 For he spake, and it was *done;* he commanded,
and it stood fast.
10 The LORD bringeth the counsel of the heathen
to nought: he maketh the devices of the people
of none effect.
11 The counsel of the LORD standeth for ever, the
thoughts of his heart to all generations.
12 Blessed *is* the nation whose God *is* the LORD;
and the people *whom* he hath chosen for his own
inheritance.

REST JOY GRACE RENEWAL

13 The LORD looketh from heaven; he beholdeth
all the sons of men.
14 From the place of his habitation he looketh
upon all the inhabitants of the earth.
15 He fashioneth their hearts alike; he consid-
ereth all their works.
16 There is no king saved by the multitude of an
host: a mighty man is not delivered by much
strength.
17 An horse *is* a vain thing for safety: neither shall
he deliver *any* by his great strength.
18 Behold, the eye of the LORD *is* upon them that
fear him, upon them that hope in his mercy;
19 To deliver their soul from death, and to keep
them alive in famine.
20 Our soul waiteth for the LORD: he *is* our help
and our shield.
21 For our heart shall rejoice in him, because we
have trusted in his holy name.
22 Let thy mercy, O LORD, be upon us, accord-
ing as we hope in thee.

Psalm 34

A Psalm *of David, when he changed his behaviour before Abimelech; who drove him away, and he departed.*

1 I will bless the LORD at all times: his praise *shall*
continually *be* in my mouth.

2 My soul shall make her boast in the LORD: the
humble shall hear *thereof*, and be glad.
3 O magnify the LORD with me, and let us exalt
his name together.
4 I sought the LORD, and he heard me, and deliv-
ered me from all my fears.
5 They looked unto him, and were lightened: and
their faces were not ashamed.
6 This poor man cried, and the LORD heard *him*,
and saved him out of all his troubles.
7 The angel of the LORD encampeth round about
them that fear him, and delivereth them.
8 O taste and see that the LORD *is* good: blessed
is the man *that* trusteth in him.
9 O fear the LORD, ye his saints: for *there is* no
want to them that fear him.
10 The young lions do lack, and suffer hunger: but
they that seek the LORD shall not want any good
thing.
11 Come, ye children, hearken unto me: I will
teach you the fear of the LORD.
12 What man *is he that* desireth life, *and* loveth
many days, that he may see good?
13 Keep thy tongue from evil, and thy lips from
speaking guile.
14 Depart from evil, and do good; seek peace, and
pursue it.

REST JOY GRACE RENEWAL

15 The eyes of the LORD *are* upon the righteous,
and his ears *are open* unto their cry.
16 The face of the LORD *is* against them that do evil,
to cut off the remembrance of them from the
earth.
17 *The righteous* cry, and the LORD heareth, and
delivereth them out of all their troubles.
18 The LORD *is* nigh unto them that are of a broken
heart; and saveth such as be of a contrite spirit.
19 Many *are* the afflictions of the righteous: but
the LORD delivereth him out of them all.
20 He keepeth all his bones: not one of them is
broken.
21 Evil shall slay the wicked: and they that hate
the righteous shall be desolate.
22 The LORD redeemeth the soul of his servants:
and none of them that trust in him shall be deso-
late.

Psalm 35

A Psalm *of David.*

1 Plead *my cause*, O LORD, with them that strive
with me: fight against them that fight against
me.
2 Take hold of shield and buckler, and stand up for
mine help.
3 Draw out also the spear, and stop *the way* against

them that persecute me: say unto my soul, I *am*
thy salvation.
4 Let them be confounded and put to shame
that seek after my soul: let them be turned back
and brought to confusion that devise my hurt.
5 Let them be as chaff before the wind: and let
the angel of the LORD chase *them.*
6 Let their way be dark and slippery: and let the
angel of the LORD persecute them.
7 For without cause have they hid for me their
net *in* a pit, *which* without cause they have digged
for my soul.
8 Let destruction come upon him at unawares;
and let his net that he hath hid catch himself:
into that very destruction let him fall.
9 And my soul shall be joyful in the LORD: it shall
rejoice in his salvation.
10 All my bones shall say, LORD, who *is* like unto
thee, which deliverest the poor from him that is
too strong for him, yea, the poor and the needy
from him that spoileth him?
11 False witnesses did rise up; they laid to my
charge *things* that I knew not.
12 They rewarded me evil for good *to* the spoiling
of my soul.
13 But as for me, when they were sick, my
clothing *was* sackcloth: I humbled my soul with

fasting; and my prayer returned into mine own
bosom.
14 I behaved myself as though *he had been* my
friend *or* brother: I bowed down heavily, as one
that mourneth *for his* mother.
15 But in mine adversity they rejoiced, and gath-
ered themselves together: *yea,* the abjects gath-
ered themselves together against me, and I knew
it not; they did tear *me,* and ceased not:
16 With hypocritical mockers in feasts, they
gnashed upon me with their teeth.
17 Lord, how long wilt thou look on? rescue my
soul from their destructions, my darling from the
lions.
18 I will give thee thanks in the great congrega-
tion: I will praise thee among much people.
19 Let not them that are mine enemies wrongful-
ly rejoice over me: *neither* let them wink with the
eye that hate me without a cause.
20 For they speak not peace: but they devise
deceitful matters against *them that are* quiet in
the land.
21 Yea, they opened their mouth wide against me,
and said, Aha, aha, our eye hath seen *it.*
22 *This* thou hast seen, O LORD: keep not silence:
O Lord, be not far from me.
23 Stir up thyself, and awake to my judgment,
even unto my cause, my God and my Lord.

24 Judge me, O LORD my God, according to thy
righteousness; and let them not rejoice over me.
25 Let them not say in their hearts, Ah, so would
we have it: let them not say, We have swallowed
him up.
26 Let them be ashamed and brought to confusion together that rejoice at mine hurt: let them be clothed with shame and dishonour that magnify *themselves* against me.
27 Let them shout for joy, and be glad, that favour my righteous cause: yea, let them say continually, Let the LORD be magnified, which hath pleasure in the prosperity of his servant.
28 And my tongue shall speak of thy righteousness *and* of thy praise all the day long.

Psalm 36

To the chief Musician,

A Psalm *of David, the servant of the* LORD.

1 The transgression of the wicked saith within my
heart, *that there is* no fear of God before his eyes.
2 For he flattereth himself in his own eyes, until
his iniquity be found to be hateful.
3 The words of his mouth *are* iniquity and deceit:
he hath left off to be wise, *and* to do good.
4 He deviseth mischief upon his bed; he setteth
himself in a way *that is* not good; he abhorreth not
evil.

5 Thy mercy, O LORD, *is* in the heavens; *and* thy
faithfulness *reacheth* unto the clouds.
6 Thy righteousness *is* like the great mountains;
thy judgments *are* a great deep: O LORD, thou
preservest man and beast.
7 How excellent *is* thy lovingkindness, O God!
therefore the children of men put their trust
under the shadow of thy wings.
8 They shall be abundantly satisfied with the fat-
ness of thy house; and thou shalt make them drink
of the river of thy pleasures.
9 For with thee *is* the fountain of life: in thy light
shall we see light.
10 O continue thy lovingkindness unto them that
know thee; and thy righteousness to the upright
in heart.
11 Let not the foot of pride come against me, and
let not the hand of the wicked remove me.
12 There are the workers of iniquity fallen: they
are cast down, and shall not be able to rise.

Psalm 37

A Psalm *of David.*

1 Fret not thyself because of evildoers, neither
be thou envious against the workers of iniquity.
2 For they shall soon be cut down like the grass,
and wither as the green herb.

3 Trust in the LORD, and do good; *so* shalt thou
dwell in the land, and verily thou shalt be fed.
4 Delight thyself also in the LORD: and he shall
give thee the desires of thine heart.
5 Commit thy way unto the LORD; trust also in
him; and he shall bring *it* to pass.
6 And he shall bring forth thy righteousness as
the light, and thy judgment as the noonday.
7 Rest in the LORD, and wait patiently for him: fret
not thyself because of him who prospereth in his
way, because of the man who bringeth wicked
devices to pass.
8 Cease from anger, and forsake wrath: fret not
thyself in any wise to do evil.
9 For evildoers shall be cut off: but those that
wait upon the LORD, they shall inherit the earth.
10 For yet a little while, and the wicked *shall* not
be: yea, thou shalt diligently consider his place,
and it *shall* not *be.*
11 But the meek shall inherit the earth; and shall
delight themselves in the abundance of peace.
12 The wicked plotteth against the just, and gnasheth
upon him with his teeth.
13 The Lord shall laugh at him: for he seeth that
his day is coming.
14 The wicked have drawn out the sword, and
have bent their bow, to cast down the poor and

needy, *and* to slay such as be of upright conver-
sation.
15 Their sword shall enter into their own heart,
and their bows shall be broken.
16 A little that a righteous man hath *is* better than
the riches of many wicked.
17 For the arms of the wicked shall be broken: but
the LORD upholdeth the righteous.
18 The LORD knoweth the days of the upright: and
their inheritance shall be for ever.
19 They shall not be ashamed in the evil time: and
in the days of famine they shall be satisfied.
20 But the wicked shall perish, and the enemies
of the LORD *shall be* as the fat of lambs: they shall
consume; into smoke shall they consume away.
21 The wicked borroweth, and payeth not again:
but the righteous sheweth mercy, and giveth.
22 For *such as be* blessed of him shall inherit the
earth; and *they that be* cursed of him shall be cut off.
23 The steps of a *good* man are ordered by the
LORD: and he delighteth in his way.
24 Though he fall, he shall not be utterly cast
down: for the LORD upholdeth *him with* his hand.
25 I have been young, and *now* am old; yet have I
not seen the righteous forsaken, nor his seed beg-
ging bread.
26 *He is* ever merciful, and lendeth; and his seed
is blessed.

27 Depart from evil, and do good; and dwell for
evermore.
28 For the LORD loveth judgment, and forsaketh
not his saints; they are preserved for ever: but the
seed of the wicked shall be cut off.
29 The righteous shall inherit the land, and dwell
therein for ever.
30 The mouth of the righteous speaketh wisdom,
and his tongue talketh of judgment.
31 The law of his God *is* in his heart; none of his
steps shall slide.
32 The wicked watcheth the righteous, and
seeketh to slay him.
33 The LORD will not leave him in his hand, nor
condemn him when he is judged.
34 Wait on the LORD, and keep his way, and he
shall exalt thee to inherit the land: when the wick-
ed are cut off, thou shalt see *it*.
35 I have seen the wicked in great power, and
spreading himself like a green bay tree.
36 Yet he passed away, and, lo, he *was* not: yea, I
sought him, but he could not be found.
37 Mark the perfect *man*, and behold the upright:
for the end of *that* man *is* peace.
38 But the transgressors shall be destroyed
together: the end of the wicked shall be cut off.
39 But the salvation of the righteous *is* of the
LORD: *he is* their strength in the time of trouble.

40 And the LORD shall help them, and deliver
them: he shall deliver them from the wicked, and
save them, because they trust in him.

Psalm 38

A Psalm of David,
to bring to remembrance.

1 O LORD, rebuke me not in thy wrath: neither
chasten me in thy hot displeasure.
2 For thine arrows stick fast in me, and thy hand
presseth me sore.
3 *There is* no soundness in my flesh because of
thine anger; neither *is there any* rest in my bones
because of my sin.
4 For mine iniquities are gone over mine head: as
an heavy burden they are too heavy for me.
5 My wounds stink *and* are corrupt because of my
foolishness.
6 I am troubled; I am bowed down greatly; I go
mourning all the day long.
7 For my loins are filled with a loathsome *disease:*
and *there is* no soundness in my flesh.
8 I am feeble and sore broken: I have roared by
reason of the disquietness of my heart.
9 Lord, all my desire *is* before thee; and my
groaning is not hid from thee.
10 My heart panteth, my strength faileth me: as
for the light of mine eyes, it also is gone from me.

11 My lovers and my friends stand aloof from my
sore; and my kinsmen stand afar off.
12 They also that seek after my life lay snares
for me: and they that seek my hurt speak mis-
chievous things, and imagine deceits all the day
long.
13 But I, as a deaf *man,* heard not; and *I was* as a
dumb man *that* openeth not his mouth.
14 Thus I was as a man that heareth not, and in
whose mouth *are* no reproofs.
15 For in thee, O LORD, do I hope: thou wilt hear,
O Lord my God.
16 For I said, *Hear me,* lest *otherwise* they should
rejoice over me: when my foot slippeth, they
magnify *themselves* against me.
17 For I *am* ready to halt, and my sorrow *is*
continually before me.
18 For I will declare mine iniquity; I will be sorry
for my sin.
19 But mine enemies *are* lively, *and* they are
strong: and they that hate me wrongfully are mul-
tiplied.
20 They also that render evil for good are mine
adversaries; because I follow *the thing that* good
is.
21 Forsake me not, O LORD: O my God, be not
far from me.
22 Make haste to help me, O Lord my salvation.

Psalm 39

To the chief Musician, even *to Jeduthun,*
A Psalm of David.

1 I said, I will take heed to my ways, that I sin not
with my tongue: I will keep my mouth with a bri-
dle, while the wicked is before me.
2 I was dumb with silence, I held my peace, *even*
from good; and my sorrow was stirred.
3 My heart was hot within me, while I was mus-
ing the fire burned: *then* spake I with my tongue,
4 LORD, make me to know mine end, and the
measure of my days, what it *is; that* I may know
how frail I *am.*
5 Behold, thou hast made my days *as* an hand-
breadth; and mine age *is* as nothing before thee:
verily every man at his best state *is* altogether
vanity. Selah.
6 Surely every man walketh in a vain shew: sure-
ly they are disquieted in vain: he heapeth up *rich-*
es, and knoweth not who shall gather them.
7 And now, Lord, what wait I for? my hope *is* in
thee.
8 Deliver me from all my transgressions: make
me not the reproach of the foolish.
9 I was dumb, I opened not my mouth; because
thou didst *it.*
10 Remove thy stroke away from me: I am con-
sumed by the blow of thine hand.

11 When thou with rebukes dost correct man for
iniquity, thou makest his beauty to consume away
like a moth: surely every man *is* vanity. Selah.
12 Hear my prayer, O LORD, and give ear unto my
cry; hold not thy peace at my tears: for I *am* a
stranger with thee, *and* a sojourner, as all my
fathers *were*.
13 O spare me, that I may recover strength,
before I go hence, and be no more.

Psalm 40

To the chief Musician, A Psalm of David.

1 I waited patiently for the LORD; and he inclined
unto me, and heard my cry.
2 He brought me up also out of an horrible pit,
out of the miry clay, and set my feet upon a rock,
and established my goings.
3 And he hath put a new song in my mouth, *even*
praise unto our God: many shall see *it*, and fear,
and shall trust in the LORD.
4 Blessed *is* that man that maketh the LORD his
trust, and respecteth not the proud, nor such as
turn aside to lies.
5 Many, O LORD my God, *are* thy wonderful
works *which* thou hast done, and thy thoughts
which are to us-ward: they cannot be reckoned up
in order unto thee: *if* I would declare and speak *of*
them, they are more than can be numbered.

6 Sacrifice and offering thou didst not desire;
mine ears hast thou opened: burnt offering and
sin offering hast thou not required.
7 Then said I, Lo, I come: in the volume of the
book *it is* written of me,
8 I delight to do thy will, O my God: yea, thy law
is within my heart.
9 I have preached righteousness in the great con-
gregation: lo, I have not refrained my lips, O LORD,
thou knowest.
10 I have not hid thy righteousness within my
heart; I have declared thy faithfulness and thy sal-
vation: I have not concealed thy lovingkindness
and thy truth from the great congregation.
11 Withhold not thou thy tender mercies from
me, O LORD: let thy lovingkindness and thy truth
continually preserve me.
12 For innumerable evils have compassed me about:
mine iniquities have taken hold upon me, so that I
am not able to look up; they are more than the hairs
of mine head: therefore my heart faileth me.
13 Be pleased, O LORD, to deliver me: O LORD,
make haste to help me.
14 Let them be ashamed and confounded together
that seek after my soul to destroy it; let them be
driven backward and put to shame that wish me evil.
15 Let them be desolate for a reward of their
shame that say unto me, Aha, aha.

16 Let all those that seek thee rejoice and be glad
in thee: let such as love thy salvation say contin-
ually, The LORD be magnified.
17 But I *am* poor and needy; *yet* the Lord thinketh
upon me: thou *art* my help and my deliverer; make
no tarrying, O my God.

Psalm 41

To the chief Musician, A Psalm of David.

1 Blessed *is* he that considereth the poor: the
LORD will deliver him in time of trouble.
2 The LORD will preserve him, and keep him alive;
and he shall be blessed upon the earth: and thou
wilt not deliver him unto the will of his enemies.
3 The LORD will strengthen him upon the bed of
languishing: thou wilt make all his bed in his sick-
ness.
4 I said, LORD, be merciful unto me: heal my soul;
for I have sinned against thee.
5 Mine enemies speak evil of me, When shall he
die, and his name perish?
6 And if he come to see *me*, he speaketh vanity:
his heart gathereth iniquity to itself; *when* he
goeth abroad, he telleth *it*.
7 All that hate me whisper together against me:
against me do they devise my hurt.
8 An evil disease, *say they*, cleaveth fast unto him:
and *now* that he lieth he shall rise up no more.

REST JOY GRACE RENEWAL

9 Yea, mine own familiar friend, in whom I trust-
ed, which did eat of my bread, hath lifted up *his*
heel against me.
10 But thou, O LORD, be merciful unto me, and
raise me up, that I may requite them.
11 By this I know that thou favourest me, because
mine enemy doth not triumph over me.
12 And as for me, thou upholdest me in mine integ-
rity, and settest me before thy face for ever.
13 Blessed *be* the LORD God of Israel from ever-
lasting, and to everlasting. Amen, and Amen.

BOOK 2

Psalm 42

To the chief Musician, Maschil,
for the sons of Korah.

1 As the hart panteth after the water brooks, so
panteth my soul after thee, O God.
2 My soul thirsteth for God, for the living God:
when shall I come and appear before God?
3 My tears have been my meat day and night, while
they continually say unto me, Where *is* thy God?
4 When I remember these *things*, I pour out my
soul in me: for I had gone with the multitude, I went
with them to the house of God, with the voice of
joy and praise, with a multitude that kept holyday.

5 Why art thou cast down, O my soul? and *why
art* thou disquieted in me? hope thou in God: for
I shall yet praise him *for* the help of his counte-
nance.
6 O my God, my soul is cast down within me:
therefore will I remember thee from the land of
Jordan, and of the Hermonites, from the hill Mizar.
7 Deep calleth unto deep at the noise of thy
waterspouts: all thy waves and thy billows are
gone over me.
8 *Yet* the LORD will command his lovingkindness in
the daytime, and in the night his song *shall be* with
me, *and* my prayer unto the God of my life.
9 I will say unto God my rock, Why hast thou for-
gotten me? why go I mourning because of the
oppression of the enemy?
10 *As* with a sword in my bones, mine enemies
reproach me; while they say daily unto me, Where
is thy God?
11 Why art thou cast down, O my soul? and why
art thou disquieted within me? hope thou in God:
for I shall yet praise him, *who is* the health of my
countenance, and my God.

Psalm 43

1 Judge me, O God, and plead my cause against
an ungodly nation: O deliver me from the deceit-
ful and unjust man.

REST JOY GRACE RENEWAL

2 For thou *art* the God of my strength: why dost
thou cast me off? why go I mourning because of
the oppression of the enemy?
3 O send out thy light and thy truth: let them
lead me; let them bring me unto thy holy hill, and
to thy tabernacles.
4 Then will I go unto the altar of God, unto God
my exceeding joy: yea, upon the harp will I praise
thee, O God my God.
5 Why art thou cast down, O my soul? and why
art thou disquieted within me? hope in God: for I
shall yet praise him, *who is* the health of my coun-
tenance, and my God.

Psalm 44

To the chief Musician for the sons of Korah, Maschil.

1 We have heard with our ears, O God, our
fathers have told us, *what* work thou didst in their
days, in the times of old.
2 *How* thou didst drive out the heathen with thy
hand, and plantedst them; *how* thou didst afflict
the people, and cast them out.
3 For they got not the land in possession by their
own sword, neither did their own arm save them:
but thy right hand, and thine arm, and the light of
thy countenance, because thou hadst a favour
unto them.

4 Thou art my King, O God: command deliver-
ances for Jacob.
5 Through thee will we push down our enemies:
through thy name will we tread them under that
rise up against us.
6 For I will not trust in my bow, neither shall my
sword save me.
7 But thou hast saved us from our enemies, and
hast put them to shame that hated us.
8 In God we boast all the day long, and praise thy
name for ever. Selah.
9 But thou hast cast off, and put us to shame; and
goest not forth with our armies.
10 Thou makest us to turn back from the enemy:
and they which hate us spoil for themselves.
11 Thou hast given us like sheep *appointed* for
meat; and hast scattered us among the heathen.
12 Thou sellest thy people for nought, and dost
not increase *thy wealth* by their price.
13 Thou makest us a reproach to our neighbours,
a scorn and a derision to them that are round
about us.
14 Thou makest us a byword among the heathen,
a shaking of the head among the people.
15 My confusion *is* continually before me, and the
shame of my face hath covered me,
16 For the voice of him that reproacheth and blas-
phemeth; by reason of the enemy and avenger.

REST JOY GRACE RENEWAL

17 All this is come upon us; yet have we not for-
gotten thee, neither have we dealt falsely in thy
covenant.
18 Our heart is not turned back, neither have our
steps declined from thy way;
19 Though thou hast sore broken us in the place of
dragons, and covered us with the shadow of death.
20 If we have forgotten the name of our God, or
stretched out our hands to a strange god;
21 Shall not God search this out? for he knoweth
the secrets of the heart.
22 Yea, for thy sake are we killed all the day long;
we are counted as sheep for the slaughter.
23 Awake, why sleepest thou, O Lord? arise, cast
us not off for ever.
24 Wherefore hidest thou thy face, *and* for-
gettest our affliction and our oppression?
25 For our soul is bowed down to the dust: our
belly cleaveth unto the earth.
26 Arise for our help, and redeem us for thy mer-
cies' sake.

Psalm 45

To the chief Musician upon Shoshannim, for the sons of Korah, Maschil, A Song of loves.

1 My heart is inditing a good matter: I speak of
the things which I have made touching the king:
my tongue *is* the pen of a ready writer.

2 Thou art fairer than the children of men: grace
is poured into thy lips: therefore God hath
blessed thee for ever.
3 Gird thy sword upon *thy* thigh, O *most* mighty,
with thy glory and thy majesty.
4 And in thy majesty ride prosperously because
of truth and meekness *and* righteousness; and
thy right hand shall teach thee terrible things.
5 Thine arrows *are* sharp in the heart of the king's
enemies; *whereby* the people fall under thee.
6 Thy throne, O God, *is* for ever and ever: the
sceptre of thy kingdom *is* a right sceptre.
7 Thou lovest righteousness, and hatest wicked-
ness: therefore God, thy God, hath anointed thee
with the oil of gladness above thy fellows.
8 All thy garments *smell* of myrrh, and aloes, *and*
cassia, out of the ivory palaces, whereby they have
made thee glad.
9 Kings' daughters *were* among thy honourable
women: upon thy right hand did stand the queen
in gold of Ophir.
10 Hearken, O daughter, and consider, and incline
thine ear; forget also thine own people, and thy
father's house;
11 So shall the king greatly desire thy beauty: for
he *is* thy Lord; and worship thou him.
12 And the daughter of Tyre *shall be there* with a gift;
even the rich among the people shall intreat thy favour.

REST JOY GRACE RENEWAL

13 The king's daughter *is* all glorious within: her
clothing *is* of wrought gold.
14 She shall be brought unto the king in raiment
of needlework: the virgins her companions that
follow her shall be brought unto thee.
15 With gladness and rejoicing shall they be
brought: they shall enter into the king's palace.
16 Instead of thy fathers shall be thy children,
whom thou mayest make princes in all the
earth.
17 I will make thy name to be remembered in all
generations: therefore shall the people praise
thee for ever and ever.

Psalm 46

To the chief Musician for the sons of Korah,
A Song upon Alamoth.

1 God *is* our refuge and strength, a very present
help in trouble.
2 Therefore will not we fear, though the earth be
removed, and though the mountains be carried
into the midst of the sea;
3 *Though* the waters thereof roar *and* be troubled,
though the mountains shake with the swelling
thereof. Selah.
4 *There is* a river, the streams whereof shall make
glad the city of God, the holy *place* of the taber-
nacles of the most High.

5 God *is* in the midst of her; she shall not be
moved: God shall help her, *and that* right early.
6 The heathen raged, the kingdoms were moved:
he uttered his voice, the earth melted.
7 The LORD of hosts *is* with us; the God of Jacob
is our refuge. Selah.
8 Come, behold the works of the LORD, what des-
olations he hath made in the earth.
9 He maketh wars to cease unto the end of the
earth; he breaketh the bow, and cutteth the spear
in sunder; he burneth the chariot in the fire.
10 Be still, and know that I *am* God: I will be exalt-
ed among the heathen, I will be exalted in the earth.
11 The LORD of hosts *is* with us; the God of Jacob
is our refuge. Selah.

Psalm 47

To the chief Musician, A Psalm for the sons of Korah.

1 O clap your hands, all ye people; shout unto
God with the voice of triumph.
2 For the LORD most high *is* terrible; *he is* a great
King over all the earth.
3 He shall subdue the people under us, and the
nations under our feet.
4 He shall choose our inheritance for us, the
excellency of Jacob whom he loved. Selah.
5 God is gone up with a shout, the LORD with the
sound of a trumpet.

REST JOY GRACE RENEWAL

6 Sing praises to God, sing praises: sing praises
unto our King, sing praises.
7 For God *is* the King of all the earth: sing ye
praises with understanding.
8 God reigneth over the heathen: God sitteth
upon the throne of his holiness.
9 The princes of the people are gathered togeth-
er, *even* the people of the God of Abraham: for
the shields of the earth *belong* unto God: he is
greatly exalted.

Psalm 48

A Song and *Psalm for the sons of Korah.*

1 Great *is* the LORD, and greatly to be praised in
the city of our God, *in* the mountain of his holi-
ness.
2 Beautiful for situation, the joy of the whole
earth, *is* mount Zion, *on* the sides of the north, the
city of the great King.
3 God is known in her palaces for a refuge.
4 For, lo, the kings were assembled, they passed
by together.
5 They saw *it, and* so they marvelled; they were
troubled, *and* hasted away.
6 Fear took hold upon them there, *and* pain, as of
a woman in travail.
7 Thou breakest the ships of Tarshish with an east
wind.

8 As we have heard, so have we seen in the city
of the LORD of hosts, in the city of our God: God
will establish it for ever. Selah.
9 We have thought of thy lovingkindness, O God,
in the midst of thy temple.
10 According to thy name, O God, so *is* thy praise
unto the ends of the earth: thy right hand is full
of righteousness.
11 Let mount Zion rejoice, let the daughters of
Judah be glad, because of thy judgments.
12 Walk about Zion, and go round about her: tell
the towers thereof.
13 Mark ye well her bulwarks, consider her palac-
es; that ye may tell *it* to the generation following.
14 For this God *is* our God for ever and ever: he
will be our guide *even* unto death.

Psalm 49

To the chief Musician, A Psalm for the sons of Korah.

1 Hear this, all *ye* people; give ear, all *ye* inhabi-
tants of the world:
2 Both low and high, rich and poor, together.
3 My mouth shall speak of wisdom; and the med-
itation of my heart *shall be* of understanding.
4 I will incline mine ear to a parable: I will open
my dark saying upon the harp.
5 Wherefore should I fear in the days of evil, *when*
the iniquity of my heels shall compass me about?

6 They that trust in their wealth, and boast them-
selves in the multitude of their riches;
7 None *of them* can by any means redeem his
brother, nor give to God a ransom for him:
8 (For the redemption of their soul *is* precious,
and it ceaseth for ever:)
9 That he should still live for ever, *and* not see
corruption.
10 For he seeth *that* wise men die, likewise the
fool and the brutish person perish, and leave their
wealth to others.
11 Their inward thought *is, that* their houses *shall*
continue for ever, *and* their dwelling places to all
generations; they call *their* lands after their own
names.
12 Nevertheless man *being* in honour abideth not:
he is like the beasts *that* perish.
13 This their way *is* their folly: yet their posterity
approve their sayings. Selah.
14 Like sheep they are laid in the grave; death
shall feed on them; and the upright shall have
dominion over them in the morning; and their
beauty shall consume in the grave from their
dwelling.
15 But God will redeem my soul from the power
of the grave: for he shall receive me. Selah.
16 Be not thou afraid when one is made rich, when
the glory of his house is increased;

17 For when he dieth he shall carry nothing away:
his glory shall not descend after him.
18 Though while he lived he blessed his soul: and
men will praise thee, when thou doest well to thy-
self.
19 He shall go to the generation of his fathers;
they shall never see light.
20 Man *that is* in honour, and understandeth not,
is like the beasts *that* perish.

Psalm 50

A Psalm of Asaph.

1 The mighty God, *even* the LORD, hath spoken,
and called the earth from the rising of the sun
unto the going down thereof.
2 Out of Zion, the perfection of beauty, God
hath shined.
3 Our God shall come, and shall not keep silence:
a fire shall devour before him, and it shall be very
tempestuous round about him.
4 He shall call to the heavens from above, and to
the earth, that he may judge his people.
5 Gather my saints together unto me; those that
have made a covenant with me by sacrifice.
6 And the heavens shall declare his righteous-
ness: for God *is* judge himself. Selah.
7 Hear, O my people, and I will speak; O Israel, and
I will testify against thee: I *am* God, *even* thy God.

8 I will not reprove thee for thy sacrifices or thy
burnt offerings, *to have been* continually before me.
9 I will take no bullock out of thy house, *nor* he
goats out of thy folds.
10 For every beast of the forest *is* mine, *and* the
cattle upon a thousand hills.
11 I know all the fowls of the mountains: and the
wild beasts of the field *are* mine.
12 If I were hungry, I would not tell thee: for the
world *is* mine, and the fulness thereof.
13 Will I eat the flesh of bulls, or drink the blood
of goats?
14 Offer unto God thanksgiving; and pay thy
vows unto the most High:
15 And call upon me in the day of trouble: I will
deliver thee, and thou shalt glorify me.
16 But unto the wicked God saith, What hast thou
to do to declare my statutes, or *that* thou should-
est take my covenant in thy mouth?
17 Seeing thou hatest instruction, and casteth my
words behind thee.
18 When thou sawest a thief, then thou con-
sentedst with him, and hast been partaker with
adulterers.
19 Thou givest thy mouth to evil, and thy tongue
frameth deceit.
20 Thou sittest *and* speakest against thy brother;
thou slanderest thine own mother's son.

21 These *things* hast thou done, and I kept silence;
thou thoughtest that I was altogether *such an one*
as thyself: *but* I will reprove thee, and set *them* in
order before thine eyes.
22 Now consider this, ye that forget God, lest I
tear *you* in pieces, and *there be* none to deliver.
23 Whoso offereth praise glorifieth me: and to
him that ordereth *his* conversation *aright* will I
shew the salvation of God.

Psalm 51

To the chief Musician, A Psalm of David, when Nathan the prophet came unto him, after he had gone in to Bath-sheba.

1 Have mercy upon me, O God, according to
thy lovingkindness: according unto the multi-
tude of thy tender mercies blot out my trans-
gressions.
2 Wash me throughly from mine iniquity, and
cleanse me from my sin.
3 For I acknowledge my transgressions: and my
sin *is* ever before me.
4 Against thee, thee only, have I sinned, and done
this evil in thy sight: that thou mightest be justi-
fied when thou speakest, *and* be clear when thou
judgest.
5 Behold, I was shapen in iniquity; and in sin did
my mother conceive me.

6 Behold, thou desirest truth in the inward parts:
and in the hidden *part* thou shalt make me to know
wisdom.
7 Purge me with hyssop, and I shall be clean: wash
me, and I shall be whiter than snow.
8 Make me to hear joy and gladness; *that* the
bones *which* thou hast broken may rejoice.
9 Hide thy face from my sins, and blot out all
mine iniquities.
10 Create in me a clean heart, O God; and renew
a right spirit within me.
11 Cast me not away from thy presence; and take
not thy holy spirit from me.
12 Restore unto me the joy of thy salvation; and
uphold me *with thy* free spirit.
13 *Then* will I teach transgressors thy ways; and
sinners shall be converted unto thee.
14 Deliver me from bloodguiltiness, O God, thou
God of my salvation: *and* my tongue shall sing
aloud of thy righteousness.
15 O Lord, open thou my lips; and my mouth shall
shew forth thy praise.
16 For thou desirest not sacrifice; else would I
give *it:* thou delightest not in burnt offering.
17 The sacrifices of God *are* a broken spirit: a bro-
ken and a contrite heart, O God, thou wilt not
despise.

18 Do good in thy good pleasure unto Zion: build
thou the walls of Jerusalem.
19 Then shalt thou be pleased with the sacrifices
of righteousness, with burnt offering and whole
burnt offering: then shall they offer bullocks upon
thine altar.

Psalm 52

To the chief Musician, Maschil, A Psalm *of David, when Doeg the Edomite came and told Saul, and said unto him, David is come to the house of Ahimelech.*

1 Why boastest thou thyself in mischief, O
mighty man? the goodness of God *endureth* continually.
2 The tongue deviseth mischiefs; like a sharp
razor, working deceitfully.
3 Thou lovest evil more than good; *and* lying rather than to speak righteousness. Selah.
4 Thou lovest all devouring words, O *thou* deceitful tongue.
5 God shall likewise destroy thee for ever, he shall
take thee away, and pluck thee out of *thy* dwelling place, and root thee out of the land of the living. Selah.
6 The righteous also shall see, and fear, and shall
laugh at him:

7 Lo, *this is* the man *that* made not God his
strength; but trusted in the abundance of his
riches, *and* strengthened himself in his wicked-
ness.
8 But I *am* like a green olive tree in the house of
God: I trust in the mercy of God for ever and ever.
9 I will praise thee for ever, because thou hast
done *it:* and I will wait on thy name; for *it is* good
before thy saints.

Psalm 53

To the chief Musician upon Mahalath, Maschil,
A Psalm *of David.*

1 The fool hath said in his heart, *There is* no God.
Corrupt are they, and have done abominable iniq-
uity: *there is* none that doeth good.
2 God looked down from heaven upon the chil-
dren of men, to see if there were *any* that did
understand, that did seek God.
3 Every one of them is gone back: they are alto-
gether become filthy; *there is* none that doeth
good, no, not one.
4 Have the workers of iniquity no knowledge?
who eat up my people *as* they eat bread: they have
not called upon God.
5 There were they in great fear, *where* no fear was:
for God hath scattered the bones of him that

encampeth *against* thee: thou hast put *them* to
shame, because God hath despised them.
6 Oh that the salvation of Israel *were come* out of
Zion! When God bringeth back the captivity of
his people, Jacob shall rejoice, *and* Israel shall be
glad.

Psalm 54

To the chief Musician on Neginoth, Maschil, A Psalm of David, when the Ziphims came and said to Saul, Doth not David hide himself with us?

1 Save me, O God, by thy name, and judge me by
thy strength.
2 Hear my prayer, O God; give ear to the words
of my mouth.
3 For strangers are risen up against me, and
oppressors seek after my soul: they have not set
God before them. Selah.
4 Behold, God *is* mine helper: the Lord *is* with
them that uphold my soul.
5 He shall reward evil unto mine enemies: cut
them off in thy truth.
6 I will freely sacrifice unto thee: I will praise thy
name, O LORD; for *it is* good.
7 For he hath delivered me out of all trouble:
and mine eye hath seen *his desire* upon mine ene-
mies.

Psalm 55

To the chief Musician on Neginoth, Maschil,
A Psalm *of David.*

1 Give ear to my prayer, O God; and hide not
thyself from my supplication.
2 Attend unto me, and hear me: I mourn in my
complaint, and make a noise;
3 Because of the voice of the enemy, because of
the oppression of the wicked: for they cast iniq-
uity upon me, and in wrath they hate me.
4 My heart is sore pained within me: and the ter-
rors of death are fallen upon me.
5 Fearfulness and trembling are come upon me,
and horror hath overwhelmed me.
6 And I said, Oh that I had wings like a dove! *for*
then would I fly away, and be at rest.
7 Lo, *then* would I wander far off, *and* remain in
the wilderness. Selah.
8 I would hasten my escape from the windy storm
and tempest.
9 Destroy, O Lord, *and* divide their tongues: for
I have seen violence and strife in the city.
10 Day and night they go about it upon the walls
thereof: mischief also and sorrow *are* in the midst
of it.
11 Wickedness *is* in the midst thereof: deceit and
guile depart not from her streets.

12 For *it was* not an enemy *that* reproached me;
then I could have borne *it:* neither *was it* he that
hated me *that* did magnify *himself* against me;
then I would have hid myself from him:
13 But *it was* thou, a man mine equal, my guide,
and mine acquaintance.
14 We took sweet counsel together, *and* walked
unto the house of God in company.
15 Let death seize upon them, *and* let them go
down quick into hell: for wickedness *is* in their
dwellings, *and* among them.
16 As for me, I will call upon God; and the LORD
shall save me.
17 Evening, and morning, and at noon, will I pray,
and cry aloud: and he shall hear my voice.
18 He hath delivered my soul in peace from the
battle *that was* against me: for there were many
with me.
19 God shall hear, and afflict them, even he that
abideth of old. Selah. Because they have no chang-
es, therefore they fear not God.
20 He hath put forth his hands against such as
be at peace with him: he hath broken his cov-
enant.
21 *The words* of his mouth were smoother than
butter, but war *was* in his heart: his words were
softer than oil, yet *were* they drawn swords.

REST JOY GRACE RENEWAL

22 Cast thy burden upon the LORD, and he shall
sustain thee: he shall never suffer the righteous
to be moved.
23 But thou, O God, shalt bring them down into
the pit of destruction: bloody and deceitful men
shall not live out half their days; but I will trust in
thee.

Psalm 56

To the chief Musician upon Jonath-elem-rechokim, Michtam of David, when the Philistines took him in Gath.

1 Be merciful unto me, O God: for man would
swallow me up; he fighting daily oppresseth me.
2 Mine enemies would daily swallow *me* up: for
they be many that fight against me, O thou most
High.
3 What time I am afraid, I will trust in thee.
4 In God I will praise his word, in God I have put
my trust; I will not fear what flesh can do unto me.
5 Every day they wrest my words: all their
thoughts *are* against me for evil.
6 They gather themselves together, they hide
themselves, they mark my steps, when they wait
for my soul.
7 Shall they escape by iniquity? in *thine* anger
cast down the people, O God.

8 Thou tellest my wanderings: put thou my tears
into thy bottle: *are they* not in thy book?
9 When I cry *unto thee*, then shall mine enemies
turn back: this I know; for God *is* for me.
10 In God will I praise *his* word: in the LORD will I
praise *his* word.
11 In God have I put my trust: I will not be afraid
what man can do unto me.
12 Thy vows *are* upon me, O God: I will render
praises unto thee.
13 For thou hast delivered my soul from death:
wilt not *thou deliver* my feet from falling, that I
may walk before God in the light of the living?

Psalm 57

To the chief Musician, Al-taschith, Michtam of David, when he fled from Saul in the cave.

1 Be merciful unto me, O God, be merciful unto
me: for my soul trusteth in thee: yea, in the shad-
ow of thy wings will I make my refuge, until *these*
calamities be overpast.
2 I will cry unto God most high; unto God that
performeth *all things* for me.
3 He shall send from heaven, and save me *from*
the reproach of him that would swallow me up.
Selah. God shall send forth his mercy and his
truth.

4 My soul *is* among lions: *and* I lie *even among*
them that are set on fire, *even* the sons of men,
whose teeth *are* spears and arrows, and their
tongue a sharp sword.
5 Be thou exalted, O God, above the heavens; *let*
thy glory *be* above all the earth.
6 They have prepared a net for my steps; my soul is
bowed down: they have digged a pit before me, into
the midst whereof they are fallen *themselves.* Selah.
7 My heart is fixed, O God, my heart is fixed: I
will sing and give praise.
8 Awake up, my glory; awake, psaltery and harp:
I *myself* will awake early.
9 I will praise thee, O Lord, among the people: I
will sing unto thee among the nations.
10 For thy mercy *is* great unto the heavens, and
thy truth unto the clouds.
11 Be thou exalted, O God, above the heavens:
let thy glory *be* above all the earth.

Psalm 58

To the chief Musician, Al-taschith, Michtam of David.
1 Do ye indeed speak righteousness, O congre-
gation? do ye judge uprightly, O ye sons of men?
2 Yea, in heart ye work wickedness; ye weigh the
violence of your hands in the earth.
3 The wicked are estranged from the womb: they
go astray as soon as they be born, speaking lies.

4 Their poison *is* like the poison of a serpent: *they*
are like the deaf adder *that* stoppeth her ear;
5 Which will not hearken to the voice of charm-
ers, charming never so wisely.
6 Break their teeth, O God, in their mouth: break
out the great teeth of the young lions, O LORD.
7 Let them melt away as waters *which* run con-
tinually: *when* he bendeth *his bow to shoot* his
arrows, let them be as cut in pieces.
8 As a snail *which* melteth, let *every one of them*
pass away: *like* the untimely birth of a woman, *that*
they may not see the sun.
9 Before your pots can feel the thorns, he shall
take them away as with a whirlwind, both living,
and in *his* wrath.
10 The righteous shall rejoice when he seeth the
vengeance: he shall wash his feet in the blood of
the wicked.
11 So that a man shall say, Verily *there is* a reward
for the righteous: verily he is a God that judgeth
in the earth.

Psalm 59

To the chief Musician, Al-taschith,
Michtam of David; when Saul sent,
and they watched the house to kill him.

1 Deliver me from mine enemies, O my God:
defend me from them that rise up against me.

2 Deliver me from the workers of iniquity, and
save me from bloody men.
3 For, lo, they lie in wait for my soul: the mighty
are gathered against me; not *for* my transgres-
sion, nor *for* my sin, O LORD.
4 They run and prepare themselves without *my*
fault: awake to help me, and behold.
5 Thou therefore, O LORD God of hosts, the God
of Israel, awake to visit all the heathen: be not
merciful to any wicked transgressors. Selah.
6 They return at evening: they make a noise like
a dog, and go round about the city.
7 Behold, they belch out with their mouth:
swords *are* in their lips: for who, *say they*, doth
hear?
8 But thou, O LORD, shalt laugh at them; thou
shalt have all the heathen in derision.
9 *Because of* his strength will I wait upon thee: for
God *is* my defence.
10 The God of my mercy shall prevent me: God
shall let me see *my desire* upon mine enemies.
11 Slay them not, lest my people forget: scatter
them by thy power; and bring them down, O Lord
our shield.
12 *For* the sin of their mouth *and* the words of
their lips let them even be taken in their pride: and
for cursing and lying *which* they speak.

13 Consume *them* in wrath, consume *them*, that
they *may* not *be:* and let them know that God
ruleth in Jacob unto the ends of the earth. Selah.
14 And at evening let them return; *and* let them
make a noise like a dog, and go round about the
city.
15 Let them wander up and down for meat, and
grudge if they be not satisfied.
16 But I will sing of thy power; yea, I will sing aloud
of thy mercy in the morning: for thou hast been
my defence and refuge in the day of my trouble.
17 Unto thee, O my strength, will I sing: for God
is my defence, *and* the God of my mercy.

Psalm 60

To the chief Musician upon Shushan-eduth,
Michtam of David,
to teach; when he strove with Aram-naharaim and with Aram-zobah, when Joab returned, and smote of Edom in the valley of salt twelve thousand.

1 O God, thou hast cast us off, thou hast scat-
tered us, thou hast been displeased; O turn thy-
self to us again.
2 Thou hast made the earth to tremble; thou hast
broken it: heal the breaches thereof; for it shaketh.
3 Thou hast shewed thy people hard things: thou
hast made us to drink the wine of astonishment.

REST JOY GRACE RENEWAL

4 Thou hast given a banner to them that fear
thee, that it may be displayed because of the
truth. Selah.
5 That thy beloved may be delivered; save *with*
thy right hand, and hear me.
6 God hath spoken in his holiness; I will rejoice, I
will divide Shechem, and mete out the valley of
Succoth.
7 Gilead *is* mine, and Manasseh *is* mine; Ephraim
also *is* the strength of mine head; Judah *is* my law-
giver;
8 Moab *is* my washpot; over Edom will I cast out
my shoe: Philistia, triumph thou because of me.
9 Who will bring me *into* the strong city? who will
lead me into Edom?
10 *Wilt* not thou, O God, *which* hadst cast us off?
and *thou,* O God, *which* didst not go out with our
armies?
11 Give us help from trouble: for vain *is* the help
of man.
12 Through God we shall do valiantly: for he *it is*
that shall tread down our enemies.

Psalm 61

To the chief Musician upon Neginah,
A Psalm *of David.*

1 Hear my cry, O God; attend unto my prayer.
2 From the end of the earth will I cry unto thee,

when my heart is overwhelmed: lead me to the
rock *that* is higher than I.
3 For thou hast been a shelter for me, *and* a
strong tower from the enemy.
4 I will abide in thy tabernacle for ever: I will trust
in the covert of thy wings. Selah.
5 For thou, O God, hast heard my vows: thou hast
given *me* the heritage of those that fear thy name.
6 Thou wilt prolong the king's life: *and* his years
as many generations.
7 He shall abide before God for ever: O prepare
mercy and truth, *which* may preserve him.
8 So will I sing praise unto thy name for ever, that
I may daily perform my vows.

Psalm 62

To the chief Musician, to Jeduthun,
A Psalm of David.

1 Truly my soul waiteth upon God: from him *com-*
eth my salvation.
2 He only *is* my rock and my salvation; *he is* my
defence; I shall not be greatly moved.
3 How long will ye imagine mischief against a
man? ye shall be slain all of you: as a bowing wall
shall ye be, and as a tottering fence.
4 They only consult to cast *him* down from his
excellency: they delight in lies: they bless with
their mouth, but they curse inwardly. Selah.

5 My soul, wait thou only upon God; for my
expectation *is* from him.
6 He only *is* my rock and my salvation: *he is* my
defence; I shall not be moved.
7 In God *is* my salvation and my glory: the rock
of my strength, *and* my refuge, *is* in God.
8 Trust in him at all times; *ye* people, pour out your
heart before him: God *is* a refuge for us. Selah.
9 Surely men of low degree *are* vanity, *and* men
of high degree *are* a lie: to be laid in the balance,
they *are* altogether *lighter* than vanity.
10 Trust not in oppression, and become not vain
in robbery: if riches increase, set not your heart
upon them.
11 God hath spoken once; twice have I heard this;
that power *belongeth* unto God.
12 Also unto thee, O Lord, *belongeth* mercy: for
thou renderest to every man according to his
work.

Psalm 63

A Psalm of David, when he was in the wilderness of Judah.

1 O God, thou *art* my God; early will I seek thee:
my soul thirsteth for thee, my flesh longeth for
thee in a dry and thirsty land, where no water is;
2 To see thy power and thy glory, so *as* I have seen
thee in the sanctuary.

3 Because thy lovingkindness *is* better than life,
my lips shall praise thee.
4 Thus will I bless thee while I live: I will lift up my
hands in thy name.
5 My soul shall be satisfied as *with* marrow and
fatness; and my mouth shall praise *thee* with joy-
ful lips:
6 When I remember thee upon my bed, *and* med-
itate on thee in the *night* watches.
7 Because thou hast been my help, therefore in
the shadow of thy wings will I rejoice.
8 My soul followeth hard after thee: thy right
hand upholdeth me.
9 But those *that* seek my soul, to destroy *it,* shall
go into the lower parts of the earth.
10 They shall fall by the sword: they shall be a por-
tion for foxes.
11 But the king shall rejoice in God; every one that
sweareth by him shall glory: but the mouth of
them that speak lies shall be stopped.

Psalm 64

To the chief Musician, A Psalm of David.

1 Hear my voice, O God, in my prayer: preserve
my life from fear of the enemy.
2 Hide me from the secret counsel of the wick-
ed; from the insurrection of the workers of iniq-
uity:

3 Who whet their tongue like a sword, *and* bend
their bows to shoot their arrows, *even* bitter words:
4 That they may shoot in secret at the perfect:
suddenly do they shoot at him, and fear not.
5 They encourage themselves *in* an evil matter:
they commune of laying snares privily; they say,
Who shall see them?
6 They search out iniquities; they accomplish a
diligent search: both the inward *thought* of every
one *of them*, and the heart, *is* deep.
7 But God shall shoot at them *with* an arrow; sud-
denly shall they be wounded.
8 So they shall make their own tongue to fall
upon themselves: all that see them shall flee away.
9 And all men shall fear, and shall declare the
work of God; for they shall wisely consider of his
doing.
10 The righteous shall be glad in the LORD, and
shall trust in him; and all the upright in heart shall
glory.

Psalm 65

To the chief Musician,
A Psalm and *Song of David.*

1 Praise waiteth for thee, O God, in Sion: and
unto thee shall the vow be performed.
2 O thou that hearest prayer, unto thee shall all
flesh come.

3 Iniquities prevail against me: *as for* our trans-
gressions, thou shalt purge them away.
4 Blessed *is the man whom* thou choosest, and
causest to approach *unto thee, that* he may dwell
in thy courts: we shall be satisfied with the good-
ness of thy house, *even* of thy holy temple.
5 By terrible things in righteousness wilt thou
answer us, O God of our salvation; *who art* the
confidence of all the ends of the earth, and of
them that are afar off *upon* the sea:
6 Which by his strength setteth fast the moun-
tains; *being* girded with power:
7 Which stilleth the noise of the seas, the noise
of their waves, and the tumult of the people.
8 They also that dwell in the uttermost parts are
afraid at thy tokens: thou makest the outgoings
of the morning and evening to rejoice.
9 Thou visitest the earth, and waterest it: thou
greatly enrichest it with the river of God, *which* is
full of water: thou preparest them corn, when
thou hast so provided for it.
10 Thou waterest the ridges thereof abundantly:
thou settlest the furrows thereof: thou makest it soft
with showers: thou blessest the springing thereof.
11 Thou crownest the year with thy goodness; and
thy paths drop fatness.
12 They drop *upon* the pastures of the wilderness:
and the little hills rejoice on every side.

13 The pastures are clothed with flocks; the val-
leys also are covered over with corn; they shout
for joy, they also sing.

Psalm 66

To the chief Musician, A Song or Psalm.

1 Make a joyful noise unto God, all ye lands:
2 Sing forth the honour of his name: make his
praise glorious.
3 Say unto God, How terrible *art thou in* thy
works! through the greatness of thy power shall
thine enemies submit themselves unto thee.
4 All the earth shall worship thee, and shall sing
unto thee; they shall sing *to* thy name. Selah.
5 Come and see the works of God: *he is* terrible
in his doing toward the children of men.
6 He turned the sea into dry *land:* they went
through the flood on foot: there did we rejoice in
him.
7 He ruleth by his power for ever; his eyes behold
the nations: let not the rebellious exalt them-
selves. Selah.
8 O bless our God, ye people, and make the voice
of his praise to be heard:
9 Which holdeth our soul in life, and suffereth
not our feet to be moved.
10 For thou, O God, hast proved us: thou hast
tried us, as silver is tried.

11 Thou broughtest us into the net; thou laidst
affliction upon our loins.
12 Thou hast caused men to ride over our heads;
we went through fire and through water: but thou
broughtest us out into a wealthy *place.*
13 I will go into thy house with burnt offerings: I
will pay thee my vows,
14 Which my lips have uttered, and my mouth
hath spoken, when I was in trouble.
15 I will offer unto thee burnt sacrifices of fat-
lings, with the incense of rams; I will offer bullocks
with goats. Selah.
16 Come *and* hear, all ye that fear God, and I will
declare what he hath done for my soul.
17 I cried unto him with my mouth, and he was
extolled with my tongue.
18 If I regard iniquity in my heart, the Lord will
not hear *me:*
19 *But* verily God hath heard *me;* he hath attend-
ed to the voice of my prayer.
20 Blessed *be* God, which hath not turned away
my prayer, nor his mercy from me.

Psalm 67

To the chief Musician on Neginoth,
A Psalm or Song.

1 God be merciful unto us, and bless us; *and* cause
his face to shine upon us; Selah.

2 That thy way may be known upon earth, thy
saving health among all nations.
3 Let the people praise thee, O God; let all the
people praise thee.
4 O let the nations be glad and sing for joy: for
thou shalt judge the people righteously, and gov-
ern the nations upon earth. Selah.
5 Let the people praise thee, O God; let all the
people praise thee.
6 *Then* shall the earth yield her increase; *and* God,
even our own God, shall bless us.
7 God shall bless us; and all the ends of the earth
shall fear him.

Psalm 68

To the chief Musician, A Psalm or Song of David.

1 Let God arise, let his enemies be scattered: let
them also that hate him flee before him.
2 As smoke is driven away, *so* drive *them* away: as
wax melteth before the fire, *so* let the wicked per-
ish at the presence of God.
3 But let the righteous be glad; let them rejoice
before God: yea, let them exceedingly rejoice.
4 Sing unto God, sing praises to his name: extol
him that rideth upon the heavens by his name JAH,
and rejoice before him.
5 A father of the fatherless, and a judge of the
widows, *is* God in his holy habitation.

6 God setteth the solitary in families: he bringeth
out those which are bound with chains: but the
rebellious dwell in a dry *land.*
7 O God, when thou wentest forth before thy
people, when thou didst march through the wil-
derness; Selah:
8 The earth shook, the heavens also dropped at
the presence of God: *even* Sinai itself *was moved*
at the presence of God, the God of Israel.
9 Thou, O God, didst send a plentiful rain, where-
by thou didst confirm thine inheritance, when it
was weary.
10 Thy congregation hath dwelt therein: thou, O
God, hast prepared of thy goodness for the poor.
11 The Lord gave the word: great *was* the compa-
ny of those that published *it.*
12 Kings of armies did flee apace: and she that
tarried at home divided the spoil.
13 Though ye have lien among the pots, *yet shall*
ye be as the wings of a dove covered with silver,
and her feathers with yellow gold.
14 When the Almighty scattered kings in it, it was
white as snow in Salmon.
15 The hill of God *is as* the hill of Bashan; an high
hill *as* the hill of Bashan.
16 Why leap ye, ye high hills? *this is* the hill *which*
God desireth to dwell in; yea, the LORD will dwell
in it for ever.

17 The chariots of God *are* twenty thousand, *even*
thousands of angels: the Lord *is* among them, *as*
in Sinai, in the holy *place.*
18 Thou hast ascended on high, thou hast led cap-
tivity captive: thou hast received gifts for men;
yea, *for* the rebellious also, that the LORD God
might dwell *among them.*
19 Blessed *be* the Lord, *who* daily loadeth us *with*
benefits, even the God of our salvation. Selah.
20 *He that is* our God *is* the God of salvation; and
unto GOD the Lord *belong* the issues from death.
21 But God shall wound the head of his enemies,
and the hairy scalp of such an one as goeth on still
in his trespasses.
22 The Lord said, I will bring again from Bashan, I will
bring *my people* again from the depths of the sea:
23 That thy foot may be dipped in the blood of *thine*
enemies, *and* the tongue of thy dogs in the same.
24 They have seen thy goings, O God; *even* the
goings of my God, my King, in the sanctuary.
25 The singers went before, the players on instru-
ments *followed* after; among *them were* the dam-
sels playing with timbrels.
26 Bless ye God in the congregations, *even* the
Lord, from the fountain of Israel.
27 There *is* little Benjamin *with* their ruler, the
princes of Judah *and* their council, the princes of
Zebulun, *and* the princes of Naphtali.

28 Thy God hath commanded thy strength:
strengthen, O God, that which thou hast wrought
for us.
29 Because of thy temple at Jerusalem shall kings
bring presents unto thee.
30 Rebuke the company of spearmen, the mul-
titude of the bulls, with the calves of the peo-
ple, *till every one* submit himself with pieces of
silver: scatter thou the people *that* delight in
war.
31 Princes shall come out of Egypt; Ethiopia shall
soon stretch out her hands unto God.
32 Sing unto God, ye kingdoms of the earth;
O sing praises unto the Lord; Selah:
33 To him that rideth upon the heavens of heav-
ens, *which were* of old; lo, he doth send out his
voice, *and that* a mighty voice.
34 Ascribe ye strength unto God: his excellency
is over Israel, and his strength *is* in the clouds.
35 O God, *thou art* terrible out of thy holy plac-
es: the God of Israel *is* he that giveth strength and
power unto *his* people. Blessed *be* God.

Psalm 69

To chief Musician upon Shoshannim,
A Psalm *of David.*

1 Save me, O God; for the waters are come in
unto *my* soul.

2 I sink in deep mire, where *there is* no standing:
I am come into deep waters, where the floods
overflow me.
3 I am weary of my crying: my throat is dried:
mine eyes fail while I wait for my God.
4 They that hate me without a cause are more than
the hairs of mine head: they that would destroy me,
being mine enemies wrongfully, are mighty: then I
restored *that* which I took not away.
5 O God, thou knowest my foolishness; and my
sins are not hid from thee.
6 Let not them that wait on thee, O Lord GOD of
hosts, be ashamed for my sake: let not those that
seek thee be confounded for my sake, O God of
Israel.
7 Because for thy sake I have borne reproach;
shame hath covered my face.
8 I am become a stranger unto my brethren, and
an alien unto my mother's children.
9 For the zeal of thine house hath eaten me up;
and the reproaches of them that reproached thee
are fallen upon me.
10 When I wept, *and chastened* my soul with fast-
ing, that was to my reproach.
11 I made sackcloth also my garment; and I
became a proverb to them.
12 They that sit in the gate speak against me; and
I *was* the song of the drunkards.

13 But as for me, my prayer *is* unto thee, O LORD,
in an acceptable time: O God, in the multitude of
thy mercy hear me, in the truth of thy salvation.
14 Deliver me out of the mire, and let me not sink:
let me be delivered from them that hate me, and
out of the deep waters.
15 Let not the waterflood overflow me, neither
let the deep swallow me up, and let not the pit
shut her mouth upon me.
16 Hear me, O LORD; for thy lovingkindness *is*
good: turn unto me according to the multitude of
thy tender mercies.
17 And hide not thy face from thy servant; for I
am in trouble: hear me speedily.
18 Draw nigh unto my soul, *and* redeem it: deliv-
er me because of mine enemies.
19 Thou hast known my reproach, and my shame,
and my dishonour: mine adversaries *are* all before
thee.
20 Reproach hath broken my heart; and I am full
of heaviness: and I looked *for some* to take pity,
but *there was* none; and for comforters, but I
found none.
21 They gave me also gall for my meat; and in my
thirst they gave me vinegar to drink.
22 Let their table become a snare before them:
and *that which should have been* for *their* welfare,
let it become a trap.

23 Let their eyes be darkened, that they see not;
and make their loins continually to shake.
24 Pour out thine indignation upon them, and let
thy wrathful anger take hold of them.
25 Let their habitation be desolate; *and* let none
dwell in their tents.
26 For they persecute *him* whom thou hast smit-
ten; and they talk to the grief of those whom thou
hast wounded.
27 Add iniquity unto their iniquity: and let them
not come into thy righteousness.
28 Let them be blotted out of the book of the liv-
ing, and not be written with the righteous.
29 But I *am* poor and sorrowful: let thy salvation,
O God, set me up on high.
30 I will praise the name of God with a song, and
will magnify him with thanksgiving.
31 *This* also shall please the LORD better than an
ox *or* bullock that hath horns and hoofs.
32 The humble shall see *this, and* be glad: and your
heart shall live that seek God.
33 For the LORD heareth the poor, and despiseth
not his prisoners.
34 Let the heaven and earth praise him, the seas,
and every thing that moveth therein.
35 For God will save Zion, and will build the cities
of Judah: that they may dwell there, and have it
in possession.

36 The seed also of his servants shall inherit it: and
they that love his name shall dwell therein.

Psalm 70

To the chief Musician, A Psalm of David,
to bring to remembrance.

1 *Make haste,* O God, to deliver me; make haste
to help me, O LORD.
2 Let them be ashamed and confounded that
seek after my soul: let them be turned backward,
and put to confusion, that desire my hurt.
3 Let them be turned back for a reward of their
shame that say, Aha, aha.
4 Let all those that seek thee rejoice and be glad
in thee: and let such as love thy salvation say con-
tinually, Let God be magnified.
5 But I *am* poor and needy: make haste unto me,
O God: thou *art* my help and my deliverer; O
LORD, make no tarrying.

Psalm 71

1 In thee, O LORD, do I put my trust: let me never
be put to confusion.
2 Deliver me in thy righteousness, and cause me
to escape: incline thine ear unto me, and save me.
3 Be thou my strong habitation, whereunto I may
continually resort: thou hast given commandment
to save me; for thou *art* my rock and my fortress.

4 Deliver me, O my God, out of the hand of the
wicked, out of the hand of the unrighteous and
cruel man.
5 For thou *art* my hope, O Lord GOD: *thou art* my
trust from my youth.
6 By thee have I been holden up from the womb:
thou art he that took me out of my mother's
bowels: my praise *shall be* continually of thee.
7 I am as a wonder unto many; but thou *art* my
strong refuge.
8 Let my mouth be filled *with* thy praise *and with*
thy honour all the day.
9 Cast me not off in the time of old age; forsake
me not when my strength faileth.
10 For mine enemies speak against me; and
they that lay wait for my soul take counsel
together,
11 Saying, God hath forsaken him: persecute and
take him; for *there is* none to deliver *him.*
12 O God, be not far from me: O my God, make
haste for my help.
13 Let them be confounded *and* consumed
that are adversaries to my soul; let them be cov-
ered *with* reproach and dishonour that seek my
hurt.
14 But I will hope continually, and will yet praise
thee more and more.

15 My mouth shall shew forth thy righteousness
and thy salvation all the day; for I know not the
numbers *thereof*.
16 I will go in the strength of the Lord GOD: I will
make mention of thy righteousness, *even* of thine
only.
17 O God, thou hast taught me from my youth:
and hitherto have I declared thy wondrous works.
18 Now also when I am old and greyheaded, O
God, forsake me not; until I have shewed thy
strength unto *this* generation, *and* thy power to
every one *that* is to come.
19 Thy righteousness also, O God, *is* very high, who
hast done great things: O God, who *is* like unto thee!
20 *Thou*, which hast shewed me great and sore
troubles, shalt quicken me again, and shalt bring
me up again from the depths of the earth.
21 Thou shalt increase my greatness, and comfort
me on every side.
22 I will also praise thee with the psaltery, *even*
thy truth, O my God: unto thee will I sing with the
harp, O thou Holy One of Israel.
23 My lips shall greatly rejoice when I sing unto
thee; and my soul, which thou hast redeemed.
24 My tongue also shall talk of thy righteousness
all the day long: for they are confounded, for they
are brought unto shame, that seek my hurt.

REST JOY GRACE RENEWAL

Psalm 72

A Psalm *for Solomon.*

1 Give the king thy judgments, O God, and thy
righteousness unto the king's son.
2 He shall judge thy people with righteousness,
and thy poor with judgment.
3 The mountains shall bring peace to the people,
and the little hills, by righteousness.
4 He shall judge the poor of the people, he shall
save the children of the needy, and shall break in
pieces the oppressor.
5 They shall fear thee as long as the sun and moon
endure, throughout all generations.
6 He shall come down like rain upon the mown
grass: as showers *that* water the earth.
7 In his days shall the righteous flourish; and
abundance of peace so long as the moon endureth.
8 He shall have dominion also from sea to sea,
and from the river unto the ends of the earth.
9 They that dwell in the wilderness shall bow
before him; and his enemies shall lick the dust.
10 The kings of Tarshish and of the isles shall bring
presents: the kings of Sheba and Seba shall offer
gifts.
11 Yea, all kings shall fall down before him: all
nations shall serve him.
12 For he shall deliver the needy when he crieth;
the poor also, and *him* that hath no helper.

PEACE | COMFORT | HOPE | STRENGTH | GRATITUDE

13 He shall spare the poor and needy, and shall
save the souls of the needy.
14 He shall redeem their soul from deceit and vio-
lence: and precious shall their blood be in his sight.
15 And he shall live, and to him shall be given of
the gold of Sheba: prayer also shall be made for
him continually; *and* daily shall he be praised.
16 There shall be an handful of corn in the earth
upon the top of the mountains; the fruit thereof
shall shake like Lebanon: and *they* of the city shall
flourish like grass of the earth.
17 His name shall endure for ever: his name shall
be continued as long as the sun: and *men* shall be
blessed in him: all nations shall call him blessed.
18 Blessed *be* the LORD God, the God of Israel,
who only doeth wondrous things.
19 And blessed *be* his glorious name for ever: and
let the whole earth be filled *with* his glory; Amen,
and Amen.
20 The prayers of David the son of Jesse are ended.

BOOK 3

Psalm 73

A Psalm of Asaph.

1 Truly God *is* good to Israel, *even* to such as are
of a clean heart.

REST JOY GRACE RENEWAL

2 But as for me, my feet were almost gone; my
steps had well nigh slipped.
3 For I was envious at the foolish, *when* I saw the
prosperity of the wicked.
4 For *there are* no bands in their death: but their
strength *is* firm.
5 They *are* not in trouble *as other* men; neither
are they plagued like *other* men.
6 Therefore pride compasseth them about as a
chain; violence covereth them *as* a garment.
7 Their eyes stand out with fatness: they have
more than heart could wish.
8 They are corrupt, and speak wickedly *concern-
ing* oppression: they speak loftily.
9 They set their mouth against the heavens, and
their tongue walketh through the earth.
10 Therefore his people return hither: and waters
of a full *cup* are wrung out to them.
11 And they say, How doth God know? and is
there knowledge in the most High?
12 Behold, these *are* the ungodly, who prosper in
the world; they increase *in* riches.
13 Verily I have cleansed my heart *in* vain, and
washed my hands in innocency.
14 For all the day long have I been plagued, and
chastened every morning.
15 If I say, I will speak thus; behold, I should offend
against the generation of thy children.

16 When I thought to know this, it *was* too pain-
ful for me;
17 Until I went into the sanctuary of God; *then*
understood I their end.
18 Surely thou didst set them in slippery places:
thou castedst them down into destruction.
19 How are they *brought* into desolation, as in a
moment! they are utterly consumed with terrors.
20 As a dream when *one* awaketh; *so,* O Lord, when
thou awakest, thou shalt despise their image.
21 Thus my heart was grieved, and I was pricked
in my reins.
22 So foolish *was* I, and ignorant: I was *as* a beast
before thee.
23 Nevertheless I *am* continually with thee: thou
hast holden *me* by my right hand.
24 Thou shalt guide me with thy counsel, and
afterward receive me *to* glory.
25 Whom have I in heaven *but thee?* and *there is*
none upon earth *that* I desire beside thee.
26 My flesh and my heart faileth: *but* God *is* the
strength of my heart, and my portion for ever.
27 For, lo, they that are far from thee shall per-
ish: thou hast destroyed all them that go a whor-
ing from thee.
28 But *it is* good for me to draw near to God: I
have put my trust in the Lord GOD, that I may
declare all thy works.

REST JOY GRACE RENEWAL

Psalm 74

Maschil of Asaph.

1 O God, why hast thou cast *us* off for ever? *why*
doth thine anger smoke against the sheep of thy
pasture?
2 Remember thy congregation, *which* thou hast
purchased of old; the rod of thine inheritance,
which thou hast redeemed; this mount Zion,
wherein thou hast dwelt.
3 Lift up thy feet unto the perpetual desolations;
even all *that* the enemy hath done wickedly in the
sanctuary.
4 Thine enemies roar in the midst of thy congre-
gations; they set up their ensigns *for* signs.
5 *A man* was famous according as he had lifted up
axes upon the thick trees.
6 But now they break down the carved work
thereof at once with axes and hammers.
7 They have cast fire into thy sanctuary, they
have defiled *by casting down* the dwelling place of
thy name to the ground.
8 They said in their hearts, Let us destroy them
together: they have burned up all the synagogues
of God in the land.
9 We see not our signs: *there is* no more any proph-
et: neither *is there* among us any that knoweth how
long.

10 O God, how long shall the adversary reproach?
shall the enemy blaspheme thy name for ever?
11 Why withdrawest thou thy hand, even thy right
hand? pluck *it* out of thy bosom.
12 For God *is* my King of old, working salvation in
the midst of the earth.
13 Thou didst divide the sea by thy strength:
thou brakest the heads of the dragons in the
waters.
14 Thou brakest the heads of leviathan in pieces,
and gavest him *to be* meat to the people inhabit-
ing the wilderness.
15 Thou didst cleave the fountain and the flood:
thou driedst up mighty rivers.
16 The day *is* thine, the night also *is* thine: thou
hast prepared the light and the sun.
17 Thou hast set all the borders of the earth: thou
hast made summer and winter.
18 Remember this, *that* the enemy hath
reproached, O LORD, and *that* the foolish people
have blasphemed thy name.
19 O deliver not the soul of thy turtledove unto
the multitude *of the wicked:* forget not the con-
gregation of thy poor for ever.
20 Have respect unto the covenant: for the dark
places of the earth are full of the habitations of cru-
elty.

REST JOY GRACE RENEWAL

21 O let not the oppressed return ashamed: let
the poor and needy praise thy name.
22 Arise, O God, plead thine own cause: remember how the foolish man reproacheth thee daily.
23 Forget not the voice of thine enemies: the
tumult of those that rise up against thee increaseth continually.

Psalm 75

To the chief Musician, Al-taschith,
A Psalm or Song of Asaph.

1 Unto thee, O God, do we give thanks, *unto thee*
do we give thanks: for *that* thy name is near thy
wondrous works declare.
2 When I shall receive the congregation I will
judge uprightly.
3 The earth and all the inhabitants thereof are
dissolved: I bear up the pillars of it. Selah.
4 I said unto the fools, Deal not foolishly: and to
the wicked, Lift not up the horn:
5 Lift not up your horn on high: speak *not with* a
stiff neck.
6 For promotion *cometh* neither from the east,
nor from the west, nor from the south.
7 But God *is* the judge: he putteth down one, and
setteth up another.
8 For in the hand of the LORD *there is* a cup, and
the wine is red; it is full of mixture; and he poureth

out of the same: but the dregs thereof, all the
wicked of the earth shall wring *them* out, *and* drink
them.
9 But I will declare for ever; I will sing praises to
the God of Jacob.
10 All the horns of the wicked also will I cut off;
but the horns of the righteous shall be exalted.

Psalm 76

To the chief Musician on Neginoth,
A Psalm or Song of Asaph.

1 In Judah *is* God known: his name *is* great in
Israel.
2 In Salem also is his tabernacle, and his dwelling
place in Zion.
3 There brake he the arrows of the bow, the
shield, and the sword, and the battle. Selah.
4 Thou *art* more glorious *and* excellent than the
mountains of prey.
5 The stouthearted are spoiled, they have slept
their sleep: and none of the men of might have
found their hands.
6 At thy rebuke, O God of Jacob, both the char-
iot and horse are cast into a dead sleep.
7 Thou, *even* thou, *art* to be feared: and who may
stand in thy sight when once thou art angry?
8 Thou didst cause judgment to be heard from
heaven; the earth feared, and was still,

9 When God arose to judgment, to save all the
meek of the earth. Selah.
10 Surely the wrath of man shall praise thee: the
remainder of wrath shalt thou restrain.
11 Vow, and pay unto the LORD your God: let all
that be round about him bring presents unto him
that ought to be feared.
12 He shall cut off the spirit of princes: *he is* ter-
rible to the kings of the earth.

Psalm 77

To the chief Musician, to Jeduthun,
A Psalm of Asaph.

1 I cried unto God with my voice, *even* unto God
with my voice; and he gave ear unto me.
2 In the day of my trouble I sought the Lord: my
sore ran in the night, and ceased not: my soul
refused to be comforted.
3 I remembered God, and was troubled: I com-
plained, and my spirit was overwhelmed. Selah.
4 Thou holdest mine eyes waking: I am so trou-
bled that I cannot speak.
5 I have considered the days of old, the years of
ancient times.
6 I call to remembrance my song in the night: I
commune with mine own heart: and my spirit
made diligent search.

7 Will the Lord cast off for ever? and will he be
favourable no more?
8 Is his mercy clean gone for ever? doth *his* prom-
ise fail for evermore?
9 Hath God forgotten to be gracious? hath he in
anger shut up his tender mercies? Selah.
10 And I said, This *is* my infirmity: *but I will remem-
ber* the years of the right hand of the most High.
11 I will remember the works of the LORD: surely
I will remember thy wonders of old.
12 I will meditate also of all thy work, and talk of
thy doings.
13 Thy way, O God, *is* in the sanctuary: who *is so*
great a God as *our* God?
14 Thou *art* the God that doest wonders: thou
hast declared thy strength among the people.
15 Thou hast with *thine* arm redeemed thy peo-
ple, the sons of Jacob and Joseph. Selah.
16 The waters saw thee, O God, the waters saw thee;
they were afraid: the depths also were troubled.
17 The clouds poured out water: the skies sent out
a sound: thine arrows also went abroad.
18 The voice of thy thunder *was* in the heaven: the
lightnings lightened the world: the earth trem-
bled and shook.
19 Thy way *is* in the sea, and thy path in the great
waters, and thy footsteps are not known.

20 Thou leddest thy people like a flock by the
hand of Moses and Aaron.

Psalm 78

Maschil of Asaph.

1 Give ear, O my people, *to* my law: incline your
ears to the words of my mouth.
2 I will open my mouth in a parable: I will utter
dark sayings of old:
3 Which we have heard and known, and our
fathers have told us.
4 We will not hide *them* from their children,
shewing to the generation to come the praises of
the LORD, and his strength, and his wonderful
works that he hath done.
5 For he established a testimony in Jacob, and
appointed a law in Israel, which he commanded
our fathers, that they should make them known
to their children:
6 That the generation to come might know *them*,
even the children *which* should be born; *who* should
arise and declare *them* to their children:
7 That they might set their hope in God, and not forget the works of God, but keep his commandments:
8 And might not be as their fathers, a stubborn
and rebellious generation; a generation *that* set
not their heart aright, and whose spirit was not
stedfast with God.

9 The children of Ephraim, *being* armed, *and* car-
rying bows, turned back in the day of battle.
10 They kept not the covenant of God, and refused
to walk in his law;
11 And forgat his works, and his wonders that he
had shewed them.
12 Marvellous things did he in the sight of their
fathers, in the land of Egypt, *in* the field of Zoan.
13 He divided the sea, and caused them to pass
through; and he made the waters to stand as an heap.
14 In the daytime also he led them with a cloud,
and all the night with a light of fire.
15 He clave the rocks in the wilderness, and gave
them drink as *out of* the great depths.
16 He brought streams also out of the rock, and
caused waters to run down like rivers.
17 And they sinned yet more against him by pro-
voking the most High in the wilderness.
18 And they tempted God in their heart by ask-
ing meat for their lust.
19 Yea, they spake against God; they said, Can
God furnish a table in the wilderness?
20 Behold, he smote the rock, that the waters
gushed out, and the streams overflowed; can he give
bread also? can he provide flesh for his people?
21 Therefore the LORD heard *this*, and was wroth:
so a fire was kindled against Jacob, and anger also
came up against Israel;

22 Because they believed not in God, and trust-
ed not in his salvation:
23 Though he had commanded the clouds from
above, and opened the doors of heaven,
24 And had rained down manna upon them to
eat, and had given them of the corn of heaven.
25 Man did eat angels' food: he sent them meat
to the full.
26 He caused an east wind to blow in the heaven:
and by his power he brought in the south wind.
27 He rained flesh also upon them as dust, and
feathered fowls like as the sand of the sea:
28 And he let *it* fall in the midst of their camp,
round about their habitations.
29 So they did eat, and were well filled: for he
gave them their own desire;
30 They were not estranged from their lust. But
while their meat *was* yet in their mouths,
31 The wrath of God came upon them, and slew
the fattest of them, and smote down the chosen
men of Israel.
32 For all this they sinned still, and believed not
for his wondrous works.
33 Therefore their days did he consume in vani-
ty, and their years in trouble.
34 When he slew them, then they sought him:
and they returned and enquired early after
God.

35 And they remembered that God *was* their
rock, and the high God their redeemer.
36 Nevertheless they did flatter him with their
mouth, and they lied unto him with their tongues.
37 For their heart was not right with him, neither
were they stedfast in his covenant.
38 But he, *being* full of compassion, forgave *their*
iniquity, and destroyed *them* not: yea, many a
time turned he his anger away, and did not stir up
all his wrath.
39 For he remembered that they *were but* flesh;
a wind that passeth away, and cometh not again.
40 How oft did they provoke him in the wilder-
ness, *and* grieve him in the desert!
41 Yea, they turned back and tempted God, and
limited the Holy One of Israel.
42 They remembered not his hand, *nor* the day
when he delivered them from the enemy.
43 How he had wrought his signs in Egypt, and
his wonders in the field of Zoan:
44 And had turned their rivers into blood; and
their floods, that they could not drink.
45 He sent divers sorts of flies among them, which
devoured them; and frogs, which destroyed them.
46 He gave also their increase unto the caterpil-
ler, and their labour unto the locust.
47 He destroyed their vines with hail, and their
sycomore trees with frost.

48 He gave up their cattle also to the hail, and
their flocks to hot thunderbolts.
49 He cast upon them the fierceness of his anger,
wrath, and indignation, and trouble, by sending
evil angels *among them.*
50 He made a way to his anger; he spared not
their soul from death, but gave their life over to
the pestilence;
51 And smote all the firstborn in Egypt; the chief
of *their* strength in the tabernacles of Ham:
52 But made his own people to go forth like sheep,
and guided them in the wilderness like a flock.
53 And he led them on safely, so that they feared
not: but the sea overwhelmed their enemies.
54 And he brought them to the border of his
sanctuary, *even to* this mountain, *which* his right
hand had purchased.
55 He cast out the heathen also before them, and
divided them an inheritance by line, and made the
tribes of Israel to dwell in their tents.
56 Yet they tempted and provoked the most high
God, and kept not his testimonies:
57 But turned back, and dealt unfaithfully like
their fathers: they were turned aside like a deceit-
ful bow.
58 For they provoked him to anger with their high
places, and moved him to jealousy with their grav-
en images.

59 When God heard *this*, he was wroth, and great-
ly abhorred Israel:
60 So that he forsook the tabernacle of Shiloh,
the tent *which* he placed among men;
61 And delivered his strength into captivity, and
his glory into the enemy's hand.
62 He gave his people over also unto the sword;
and was wroth with his inheritance.
63 The fire consumed their young men; and their
maidens were not given to marriage.
64 Their priests fell by the sword; and their wid-
ows made no lamentation.
65 Then the Lord awaked as one out of sleep, *and*
like a mighty man that shouteth by reason of
wine.
66 And he smote his enemies in the hinder parts:
he put them to a perpetual reproach.
67 Moreover he refused the tabernacle of Joseph,
and chose not the tribe of Ephraim:
68 But chose the tribe of Judah, the mount Zion
which he loved.
69 And he built his sanctuary like high *palaces*,
like the earth which he hath established for ever.
70 He chose David also his servant, and took him
from the sheepfolds:
71 From following the ewes great with young he
brought him to feed Jacob his people, and Israel
his inheritance.

72 So he fed them according to the integrity of
his heart; and guided them by the skilfulness of
his hands.

Psalm 79

A Psalm of Asaph.

1 O God, the heathen are come into thine inher-
itance; thy holy temple have they defiled; they
have laid Jerusalem on heaps.
2 The dead bodies of thy servants have they given
to be meat unto the fowls of the heaven, the flesh
of thy saints unto the beasts of the earth.
3 Their blood have they shed like water round
about Jerusalem; and *there was* none to bury *them.*
4 We are become a reproach to our neighbours,
a scorn and derision to them that are round about
us.
5 How long, LORD? wilt thou be angry for ever?
shall thy jealousy burn like fire?
6 Pour out thy wrath upon the heathen that have
not known thee, and upon the kingdoms that have
not called upon thy name.
7 For they have devoured Jacob, and laid waste
his dwelling place.
8 O remember not against us former iniquities:
let thy tender mercies speedily prevent us: for we
are brought very low.

9 Help us, O God of our salvation, for the glory
of thy name: and deliver us, and purge away our
sins, for thy name's sake.
10 Wherefore should the heathen say, Where *is*
their God? let him be known among the heathen
in our sight *by* the revenging of the blood of thy
servants *which is* shed.
11 Let the sighing of the prisoner come before
thee; according to the greatness of thy power
preserve thou those that are appointed to die;
12 And render unto our neighbours sevenfold
into their bosom their reproach, wherewith they
have reproached thee, O Lord.
13 So we thy people and sheep of thy pasture will
give thee thanks for ever: we will shew forth thy
praise to all generations.

Psalm 80

To the chief Musician upon Shoshannim-Eduth,
A Psalm of Asaph.

1 Give ear, O Shepherd of Israel, thou that leadest
Joseph like a flock; thou that dwellest *between* the
cherubims, shine forth.
2 Before Ephraim and Benjamin and Manasseh
stir up thy strength, and come *and* save us.
3 Turn us again, O God, and cause thy face to
shine; and we shall be saved.

4 O LORD God of hosts, how long wilt thou be
angry against the prayer of thy people?
5 Thou feedest them with the bread of tears; and
givest them tears to drink in great measure.
6 Thou makest us a strife unto our neighbours:
and our enemies laugh among themselves.
7 Turn us again, O God of hosts, and cause thy
face to shine; and we shall be saved.
8 Thou hast brought a vine out of Egypt: thou
hast cast out the heathen, and planted it.
9 Thou preparedst *room* before it, and didst cause
it to take deep root, and it filled the land.
10 The hills were covered with the shadow of it, and
the boughs thereof *were like* the goodly cedars.
11 She sent out her boughs unto the sea, and her
branches unto the river.
12 Why hast thou *then* broken down her hedges,
so that all they which pass by the way do pluck her?
13 The boar out of the wood doth waste it, and the
wild beast of the field doth devour it.
14 Return, we beseech thee, O God of hosts: look
down from heaven, and behold, and visit this vine;
15 And the vineyard which thy right hand hath
planted, and the branch *that* thou madest strong
for thyself.
16 *It is* burned with fire, *it is* cut down: they per-
ish at the rebuke of thy countenance.

17 Let thy hand be upon the man of thy right hand,
upon the son of man *whom* thou madest strong for
thyself.
18 So will not we go back from thee: quicken us,
and we will call upon thy name.
19 Turn us again, O LORD God of hosts, cause thy
face to shine; and we shall be saved.

Psalm 81

To the chief Musician upon Gittith,
A Psalm *of Asaph.*

1 Sing aloud unto God our strength: make a joy-
ful noise unto the God of Jacob.
2 Take a psalm, and bring hither the timbrel, the
pleasant harp with the psaltery.
3 Blow up the trumpet in the new moon, in the
time appointed, on our solemn feast day.
4 For this *was* a statute for Israel, *and* a law of the
God of Jacob.
5 This he ordained in Joseph *for* a testimony,
when he went out through the land of Egypt:
where I heard a language *that* I understood not.
6 I removed his shoulder from the burden: his
hands were delivered from the pots.
7 Thou calledst in trouble, and I delivered thee;
I answered thee in the secret place of thunder: I
proved thee at the waters of Meribah. Selah.

REST JOY GRACE RENEWAL

8 Hear, O my people, and I will testify unto thee:
O Israel, if thou wilt hearken unto me;
9 There shall no strange god be in thee; neither
shalt thou worship any strange god.
10 I *am* the LORD thy God, which brought thee
out of the land of Egypt: open thy mouth wide,
and I will fill it.
11 But my people would not hearken to my voice;
and Israel would none of me.
12 So I gave them up unto their own hearts' lust:
and they walked in their own counsels.
13 Oh that my people had hearkened unto me,
and Israel had walked in my ways!
14 I should soon have subdued their enemies,
and turned my hand against their adversaries.
15 The haters of the LORD should have submitted
themselves unto him: but their time should have
endured for ever.
16 He should have fed them also with the finest
of the wheat: and with honey out of the rock
should I have satisfied thee.

Psalm 82

A Psalm of Asaph.

1 God standeth in the congregation of the mighty;
he judgeth among the gods.
2 How long will ye judge unjustly, and accept the
persons of the wicked? Selah.

3 Defend the poor and fatherless: do justice to
the afflicted and needy.
4 Deliver the poor and needy: rid *them* out of the
hand of the wicked.
5 They know not, neither will they understand;
they walk on in darkness: all the foundations of
the earth are out of course.
6 I have said, Ye *are* gods; and all of you *are* chil-
dren of the most High.
7 But ye shall die like men, and fall like one of the
princes.
8 Arise, O God, judge the earth: for thou shalt
inherit all nations.

Psalm 83

A Song or
Psalm of Asaph.

1 Keep not thou silence, O God: hold not thy
peace, and be not still, O God.
2 For, lo, thine enemies make a tumult: and they
that hate thee have lifted up the head.
3 They have taken crafty counsel against thy
people, and consulted against thy hidden ones.
4 They have said, Come, and let us cut them off
from *being* a nation; that the name of Israel may
be no more in remembrance.
5 For they have consulted together with one
consent: they are confederate against thee:

6 The tabernacles of Edom, and the Ishmaelites;
of Moab, and the Hagarenes;
7 Gebal, and Ammon, and Amalek; the Philis-
tines with the inhabitants of Tyre;
8 Assur also is joined with them: they have hol-
pen the children of Lot. Selah.
9 Do unto them as *unto* the Midianites; as *to*
Sisera, as *to* Jabin, at the brook of Kison:
10 *Which* perished at Endor: they became *as* dung
for the earth.
11 Make their nobles like Oreb, and like Zeeb: yea,
all their princes as Zebah, and as Zalmunna:
12 Who said, Let us take to ourselves the houses
of God in possession.
13 O my God, make them like a wheel; as the
stubble before the wind.
14 As the fire burneth a wood, and as the flame
setteth the mountains on fire;
15 So persecute them with thy tempest, and
make them afraid with thy storm.
16 Fill their faces with shame; that they may seek
thy name, O LORD.
17 Let them be confounded and troubled for ever;
yea, let them be put to shame, and perish:
18 That *men* may know that thou, whose name
alone *is* JEHOVAH, *art* the most high over all the
earth.

Psalm 84

To the chief Musician upon Gittith,
A Psalm for the sons of Korah.

1 How amiable *are* thy tabernacles, O LORD of
hosts!
2 My soul longeth, yea, even fainteth for the
courts of the LORD: my heart and my flesh crieth
out for the living God.
3 Yea, the sparrow hath found an house, and the
swallow a nest for herself, where she may lay her
young, *even* thine altars, O LORD of hosts, my
King, and my God.
4 Blessed *are* they that dwell in thy house: they
will be still praising thee. Selah.
5 Blessed *is* the man whose strength *is* in thee; in
whose heart *are* the ways *of them.*
6 *Who* passing through the valley of Baca make
it a well; the rain also filleth the pools.
7 They go from strength to strength, *every one of*
them in Zion appeareth before God.
8 O LORD God of hosts, hear my prayer: give ear,
O God of Jacob. Selah.
9 Behold, O God our shield, and look upon the
face of thine anointed.
10 For a day in thy courts *is* better than a thou-
sand. I had rather be a doorkeeper in the house of
my God, than to dwell in the tents of wickedness.

REST JOY GRACE RENEWAL

11 For the LORD God *is* a sun and shield: the LORD
will give grace and glory: no good *thing* will he
withhold from them that walk uprightly.
12 O LORD of hosts, blessed *is* the man that trust-
eth in thee.

Psalm 85

To the chief Musician,
A Psalm for the sons of Korah.

1 LORD, thou hast been favourable unto thy
land: thou hast brought back the captivity of
Jacob.
2 Thou hast forgiven the iniquity of thy people,
thou hast covered all their sin. Selah.
3 Thou hast taken away all thy wrath: thou hast
turned *thyself* from the fierceness of thine
anger.
4 Turn us, O God of our salvation, and cause
thine anger toward us to cease.
5 Wilt thou be angry with us for ever? wilt thou
draw out thine anger to all generations?
6 Wilt thou not revive us again: that thy people
may rejoice in thee?
7 Shew us thy mercy, O LORD, and grant us thy
salvation.
8 I will hear what God the LORD will speak: for he
will speak peace unto his people, and to his saints:
but let them not turn again to folly.

9 Surely his salvation is nigh them that fear him;
that glory may dwell in our land.
10 Mercy and truth are met together; righteous-
ness and peace have kissed *each other.*
11 Truth shall spring out of the earth; and righ-
teousness shall look down from heaven.
12 Yea, the LORD shall give *that which is* good; and
our land shall yield her increase.
13 Righteousness shall go before him; and shall
set *us* in the way of his steps.

Psalm 86

A Prayer of David.

1 Bow down thine ear, O LORD, hear me: for I *am*
poor and needy.
2 Preserve my soul; for I *am* holy: O thou my
God, save thy servant that trusteth in thee.
3 Be merciful unto me, O Lord: for I cry unto
thee daily.
4 Rejoice the soul of thy servant: for unto thee,
O Lord, do I lift up my soul.
5 For thou, Lord, *art* good, and ready to forgive;
and plenteous in mercy unto all them that call
upon thee.
6 Give ear, O LORD, unto my prayer; and attend
to the voice of my supplications.
7 In the day of my trouble I will call upon thee:
for thou wilt answer me.

REST JOY GRACE RENEWAL

8 Among the gods *there is* none like unto thee, O
Lord; neither *are there any works* like unto thy
works.
9 All nations whom thou hast made shall come
and worship before thee, O Lord; and shall glori-
fy thy name.
10 For thou *art* great, and doest wondrous
things: thou *art* God alone.
11 Teach me thy way, O LORD; I will walk in thy
truth: unite my heart to fear thy name.
12 I will praise thee, O Lord my God, with all my
heart: and I will glorify thy name for evermore.
13 For great *is* thy mercy toward me: and thou
hast delivered my soul from the lowest hell.
14 O God, the proud are risen against me, and the
assemblies of violent *men* have sought after my
soul; and have not set thee before them.
15 But thou, O Lord, *art* a God full of compas-
sion, and gracious, longsuffering, and plenteous
in mercy and truth.
16 O turn unto me, and have mercy upon me; give
thy strength unto thy servant, and save the son
of thine handmaid.
17 Shew me a token for good; that they which
hate me may see *it*, and be ashamed: because
thou, LORD, hast holpen me, and comforted
me.

Psalm 87

A Psalm or Song for
the sons of Korah.

1 His foundation *is* in the holy mountains.
2 The LORD loveth the gates of Zion more than
all the dwellings of Jacob.
3 Glorious things are spoken of thee, O city of
God. Selah.
4 I will make mention of Rahab and Babylon to
them that know me: behold Philistia, and Tyre,
with Ethiopia; this *man* was born there.
5 And of Zion it shall be said, This and *that man*
was born in her: and the highest himself shall
establish her.
6 The LORD shall count, when he writeth up the
people, that this man was born there. Selah.
7 As well the singers as the players on instru-
ments *shall be there:* all my springs *are* in thee.

Psalm 88

A Song or Psalm for the sons of Korah, to the chief
Musician upon Mahalath Leannoth, Maschil
of Heman the Ezrahite.

1 O LORD God of my salvation, I have cried day
and night before thee:
2 Let my prayer come before thee: incline thine
ear unto my cry;

REST JOY GRACE RENEWAL

3 For my soul is full of troubles: and my life
drawteth nigh unto the grave.
4 I am counted with them that go down into the
pit: I am as a man *that hath* no strength:
5 Free among the dead, like the slain that lie in
the grave, whom thou rememberest no more: and
they are cut off from thy hand.
6 Thou hast laid me in the lowest pit, in darkness,
in the deeps.
7 Thy wrath lieth hard upon me, and thou hast
afflicted *me* with all thy waves. Selah.
8 Thou hast put away mine acquaintance far from
me; thou hast made me an abomination unto
them: *I am* shut up, and I cannot come forth.
9 Mine eye mourneth by reason of affliction:
LORD, I have called daily upon thee, I have
stretched out my hands unto thee.
10 Wilt thou shew wonders to the dead? shall the
dead arise *and* praise thee? Selah.
11 Shall thy lovingkindness be declared in the
grave? *or* thy faithfulness in destruction?
12 Shall thy wonders be known in the dark? and
thy righteousness in the land of forgetfulness?
13 But unto thee have I cried, O LORD; and in the
morning shall my prayer prevent thee.
14 LORD, why castest thou off my soul? *why* hidest
thou thy face from me?

15 I *am* afflicted and ready to die from *my* youth
up: *while* I suffer thy terrors I am distracted.
16 Thy fierce wrath goeth over me; thy terrors
have cut me off.
17 They came round about me daily like water;
they compassed me about together.
18 Lover and friend hast thou put far from me,
and mine acquaintance into darkness.

Psalm 89

Maschil of Ethan the Ezrahite.

1 I will sing of the mercies of the LORD for ever:
with my mouth will I make known thy faithfulness
to all generations.
2 For I have said, Mercy shall be built up for ever:
thy faithfulness shalt thou establish in the very
heavens.
3 I have made a covenant with my chosen, I have
sworn unto David my servant,
4 Thy seed will I establish for ever, and build up
thy throne to all generations. Selah.
5 And the heavens shall praise thy wonders, O
LORD: thy faithfulness also in the congregation of
the saints.
6 For who in the heaven can be compared unto
the LORD? *who* among the sons of the mighty can
be likened unto the LORD?

7 God is greatly to be feared in the assembly of
the saints, and to be had in reverence of all *them*
that are about him.
8 O LORD God of hosts, who *is* a strong LORD like
unto thee? or to thy faithfulness round about thee?
9 Thou rulest the raging of the sea: when the
waves thereof arise, thou stillest them.
10 Thou hast broken Rahab in pieces, as one that
is slain; thou hast scattered thine enemies with
thy strong arm.
11 The heavens *are* thine, the earth also *is* thine:
as for the world and the fulness thereof, thou hast
founded them.
12 The north and the south thou hast created them:
Tabor and Hermon shall rejoice in thy name.
13 Thou hast a mighty arm: strong is thy hand, *and*
high is thy right hand.
14 Justice and judgment *are* the habitation of thy
throne: mercy and truth shall go before thy face.
15 Blessed *is* the people that know the joyful
sound: they shall walk, O LORD, in the light of thy
countenance.
16 In thy name shall they rejoice all the day: and
in thy righteousness shall they be exalted.
17 For thou *art* the glory of their strength: and in
thy favour our horn shall be exalted.
18 For the LORD *is* our defence; and the Holy One
of Israel *is* our king.

19 Then thou spakest in vision to thy holy one, and
saidst, I have laid help upon *one that is* mighty; I
have exalted *one* chosen out of the people.
20 I have found David my servant; with my holy
oil have I anointed him:
21 With whom my hand shall be established: mine
arm also shall strengthen him.
22 The enemy shall not exact upon him; nor the
son of wickedness afflict him.
23 And I will beat down his foes before his face,
and plague them that hate him.
24 But my faithfulness and my mercy *shall be*
with him: and in my name shall his horn be exalt-
ed.
25 I will set his hand also in the sea, and his right
hand in the rivers.
26 He shall cry unto me, Thou *art* my father, my
God, and the rock of my salvation.
27 Also I will make him *my* firstborn, higher than
the kings of the earth.
28 My mercy will I keep for him for evermore, and
my covenant shall stand fast with him.
29 His seed also will I make *to endure* for ever, and
his throne as the days of heaven.
30 If his children forsake my law, and walk not in
my judgments;
31 If they break my statutes, and keep not my
commandments;

32 Then will I visit their transgression with the rod,
and their iniquity with stripes.
33 Nevertheless my lovingkindness will I not utter-
ly take from him, nor suffer my faithfulness to fail.
34 My covenant will I not break, nor alter the
thing that is gone out of my lips.
35 Once have I sworn by my holiness that I will
not lie unto David.
36 His seed shall endure for ever, and his throne
as the sun before me.
37 It shall be established for ever as the moon, and
as a faithful witness in heaven. Selah.
38 But thou hast cast off and abhorred, thou hast
been wroth with thine anointed.
39 Thou hast made void the covenant of thy ser-
vant: thou hast profaned his crown *by casting it* to
the ground.
40 Thou hast broken down all his hedges; thou
hast brought his strong holds to ruin.
41 All that pass by the way spoil him: he is a
reproach to his neighbours.
42 Thou hast set up the right hand of his adver-
saries; thou hast made all his enemies to rejoice.
43 Thou hast also turned the edge of his sword,
and hast not made him to stand in the battle.
44 Thou hast made his glory to cease, and cast his
throne down to the ground.

45 The days of his youth hast thou shortened:
thou hast covered him with shame. Selah.
46 How long, LORD? wilt thou hide thyself for
ever? shall thy wrath burn like fire?
47 Remember how short my time is: wherefore
hast thou made all men in vain?
48 What man *is he that* liveth, and shall not see
death? shall he deliver his soul from the hand of
the grave? Selah.
49 Lord, where *are* thy former lovingkindnesses,
which thou swarest unto David in thy truth?
50 Remember, Lord, the reproach of thy ser-
vants; *how* I do bear in my bosom *the reproach of*
all the mighty people;
51 Wherewith thine enemies have reproached, O
LORD; wherewith they have reproached the foot-
steps of thine anointed.
52 Blessed *be* the LORD for evermore. Amen, and
Amen.

BOOK 4

Psalm 90

A Prayer of Moses the man of God.

1 Lord, thou hast been our dwelling place in all
generations.

2 Before the mountains were brought forth, or
ever thou hadst formed the earth and the world,
even from everlasting to everlasting, thou *art*
God.
3 Thou turnest man to destruction; and sayest,
Return, ye children of men.
4 For a thousand years in thy sight *are but* as yes-
terday when it is past, and *as* a watch in the night.
5 Thou carriest them away as with a flood; they
are *as* a sleep: in the morning *they are* like grass
which groweth up.
6 In the morning it flourisheth, and groweth up;
in the evening it is cut down, and withereth.
7 For we are consumed by thine anger, and by thy
wrath are we troubled.
8 Thou hast set our iniquities before thee, our
secret *sins* in the light of thy countenance.
9 For all our days are passed away in thy wrath:
we spend our years as a tale *that is told*.
10 The days of our years *are* threescore years and
ten; and if by reason of strength *they be* fourscore
years, yet *is* their strength labour and sorrow; for
it is soon cut off, and we fly away.
11 Who knoweth the power of thine anger? even
according to thy fear, *so is* thy wrath.
12 So teach *us* to number our days, that we may
apply *our* hearts unto wisdom.

13 Return, O LORD, how long? and let it repent
thee concerning thy servants.
14 O satisfy us early with thy mercy; that we may
rejoice and be glad all our days.
15 Make us glad according to the days *wherein*
thou hast afflicted us, *and* the years *wherein* we
have seen evil.
16 Let thy work appear unto thy servants, and thy
glory unto their children.
17 And let the beauty of the LORD our God be
upon us: and establish thou the work of our hands
upon us; yea, the work of our hands establish thou
it.

Psalm 91

1 He that dwelleth in the secret place of the most
High shall abide under the shadow of the
Almighty.
2 I will say of the LORD, *He is* my refuge and my
fortress: my God; in him will I trust.
3 Surely he shall deliver thee from the snare of
the fowler, *and* from the noisome pestilence.
4 He shall cover thee with his feathers, and under
his wings shalt thou trust: his truth *shall be thy*
shield and buckler.
5 Thou shalt not be afraid for the terror by night;
nor for the arrow *that* flieth by day;

6 *Nor* for the pestilence *that* walketh in dark-
ness; *nor* for the destruction *that* wasteth at
noonday.
7 A thousand shall fall at thy side, and ten thou-
sand at thy right hand; *but* it shall not come nigh
thee.
8 Only with thine eyes shalt thou behold and see
the reward of the wicked.
9 Because thou hast made the LORD, *which is* my
refuge, *even* the most High, thy habitation;
10 There shall no evil befall thee, neither shall any
plague come nigh thy dwelling.
11 For he shall give his angels charge over thee, to
keep thee in all thy ways.
12 They shall bear thee up in *their* hands, lest thou
dash thy foot against a stone.
13 Thou shalt tread upon the lion and adder: the
young lion and the dragon shalt thou trample
under feet.
14 Because he hath set his love upon me, there-
fore will I deliver him: I will set him on high,
because he hath known my name.
15 He shall call upon me, and I will answer him: I
will be with him in trouble; I will deliver him, and
honour him.
16 With long life will I satisfy him, and shew him
my salvation.

Psalm 92

A Psalm or Song for the sabbath day.

1 *It is a* good *thing* to give thanks unto the LORD,
and to sing praises unto thy name, O most
High:
2 To shew forth thy lovingkindness in the morn-
ing, and thy faithfulness every night,
3 Upon an instrument of ten strings, and upon
the psaltery; upon the harp with a solemn sound.
4 For thou, LORD, hast made me glad through thy
work: I will triumph in the works of thy hands.
5 O LORD, how great are thy works! *and* thy
thoughts are very deep.
6 A brutish man knoweth not; neither doth a fool
understand this.
7 When the wicked spring as the grass, and when
all the workers of iniquity do flourish; *it is* that
they shall be destroyed for ever:
8 But thou, LORD, *art most* high for evermore.
9 For, lo, thine enemies, O LORD, for, lo, thine
enemies shall perish; all the workers of iniquity
shall be scattered.
10 But my horn shalt thou exalt like *the horn of* an
unicorn: I shall be anointed with fresh oil.
11 Mine eye also shall see *my desire* on mine ene-
mies, *and* mine ears shall hear *my desire* of the
wicked that rise up against me.

REST JOY GRACE RENEWAL

12 The righteous shall flourish like the palm tree:
he shall grow like a cedar in Lebanon.
13 Those that be planted in the house of the LORD
shall flourish in the courts of our God.
14 They shall still bring forth fruit in old age; they
shall be fat and flourishing;
15 To shew that the LORD *is* upright: *he is* my rock,
and *there is* no unrighteousness in him.

Psalm 93

1 The LORD reigneth, he is clothed with majesty;
the LORD is clothed with strength, *wherewith* he
hath girded himself: the world also is stablished,
that it cannot be moved.
2 Thy throne *is* established of old: thou *art* from
everlasting.
3 The floods have lifted up, O LORD, the floods
have lifted up their voice; the floods lift up their
waves.
4 The LORD on high *is* mightier than the noise of
many waters, *yea, than* the mighty waves of the sea.
5 Thy testimonies are very sure: holiness becom-
eth thine house, O LORD, for ever.

Psalm 94

1 O LORD God, to whom vengeance belongeth;
O God, to whom vengeance belongeth, shew thy-
self.

2 Lift up thyself, thou judge of the earth: render
a reward to the proud.
3 LORD, how long shall the wicked, how long shall
the wicked triumph?
4 *How long* shall they utter *and* speak hard things?
and all the workers of iniquity boast themselves?
5 They break in pieces thy people, O LORD, and
afflict thine heritage.
6 They slay the widow and the stranger, and mur-
der the fatherless.
7 Yet they say, The LORD shall not see, neither
shall the God of Jacob regard *it*.
8 Understand, ye brutish among the people: and
ye fools, when will ye be wise?
9 He that planted the ear, shall he not hear? he
that formed the eye, shall he not see?
10 He that chastiseth the heathen, shall not he
correct? he that teacheth man knowledge, *shall
not he know?*
11 The LORD knoweth the thoughts of man, that
they *are* vanity.
12 Blessed *is* the man whom thou chastenest, O
LORD, and teachest him out of thy law;
13 That thou mayest give him rest from the days
of adversity, until the pit be digged for the wick-
ed.
14 For the LORD will not cast off his people, nei-
ther will he forsake his inheritance.

REST JOY GRACE RENEWAL

15 But judgment shall return unto righteousness:
and all the upright in heart shall follow it.
16 Who will rise up for me against the evildoers? *or*
who will stand up for me against the workers of
iniquity?
17 Unless the LORD *had been* my help, my soul had
almost dwelt in silence.
18 When I said, My foot slippeth; thy mercy, O
LORD, held me up.
19 In the multitude of my thoughts within me thy
comforts delight my soul.
20 Shall the throne of iniquity have fellowship
with thee, which frameth mischief by a law?
21 They gather themselves together against the soul
of the righteous, and condemn the innocent blood.
22 But the LORD is my defence; and my God *is*
the rock of my refuge.
23 And he shall bring upon them their own iniq-
uity, and shall cut them off in their own wicked-
ness; *yea*, the LORD our God shall cut them off.

Psalm 95

1 O come, let us sing unto the LORD: let us make
a joyful noise to the rock of our salvation.
2 Let us come before his presence with thanksgiv-
ing, and make a joyful noise unto him with psalms.
3 For the LORD *is* a great God, and a great King
above all gods.

4 In his hand *are* the deep places of the earth: the
strength of the hills *is* his also.
5 The sea *is* his, and he made it: and his hands
formed the dry *land*.
6 O come, let us worship and bow down: let us
kneel before the LORD our maker.
7 For he *is* our God; and we *are* the people of his
pasture, and the sheep of his hand. To day if ye will
hear his voice,
8 Harden not your heart, as in the provocation,
and as *in* the day of temptation in the wilderness:
9 When your fathers tempted me, proved me,
and saw my work.
10 Forty years long was I grieved with *this* gener-
ation, and said, It *is* a people that do err in their
heart, and they have not known my ways:
11 Unto whom I sware in my wrath that they
should not enter into my rest.

Psalm 96

1 O sing unto the LORD a new song: sing unto the
LORD, all the earth.
2 Sing unto the LORD, bless his name; shew forth
his salvation from day to day.
3 Declare his glory among the heathen, his won-
ders among all people.
4 For the LORD *is* great, and greatly to be praised:
he *is* to be feared above all gods.

5 For all the gods of the nations *are* idols: but the
LORD made the heavens.
6 Honour and majesty *are* before him: strength
and beauty *are* in his sanctuary.
7 Give unto the LORD, O ye kindreds of the peo-
ple, give unto the LORD glory and strength.
8 Give unto the LORD the glory *due unto* his
name: bring an offering, and come into his courts.
9 O worship the LORD in the beauty of holiness:
fear before him, all the earth.
10 Say among the heathen *that* the LORD
reigneth: the world also shall be established that
it shall not be moved: he shall judge the people
righteously.
11 Let the heavens rejoice, and let the earth be
glad; let the sea roar, and the fulness thereof.
12 Let the field be joyful, and all that *is* therein:
then shall all the trees of the wood rejoice
13 Before the LORD: for he cometh, for he com-
eth to judge the earth: he shall judge the world
with righteousness, and the people with his truth.

Psalm 97

1 The LORD reigneth; let the earth rejoice; let the
multitude of isles be glad *thereof*.
2 Clouds and darkness *are* round about him: righ-
teousness and judgment *are* the habitation of his
throne.

3 A fire goeth before him, and burneth up his
enemies round about.
4 His lightnings enlightened the world: the earth
saw, and trembled.
5 The hills melted like wax at the presence of the
LORD, at the presence of the Lord of the whole earth.
6 The heavens declare his righteousness, and all
the people see his glory.
7 Confounded be all they that serve graven imag-
es, that boast themselves of idols: worship him, all
ye gods.
8 Zion heard, and was glad; and the daughters of
Judah rejoiced because of thy judgments, O LORD.
9 For thou, LORD, *art* high above all the earth:
thou art exalted far above all gods.
10 Ye that love the LORD, hate evil: he preserveth
the souls of his saints; he delivereth them out of
the hand of the wicked.
11 Light is sown for the righteous, and gladness
for the upright in heart.
12 Rejoice in the LORD, ye righteous; and give
thanks at the remembrance of his holiness.

Psalm 98

A Psalm.

1 O sing unto the LORD a new song; for he hath
done marvellous things: his right hand, and his
holy arm, hath gotten him the victory.

2 The LORD hath made known his salvation: his
righteousness hath he openly shewed in the sight
of the heathen.
3 He hath remembered his mercy and his truth
toward the house of Israel: all the ends of the
earth have seen the salvation of our God.
4 Make a joyful noise unto the LORD, all the earth:
make a loud noise, and rejoice, and sing praise.
5 Sing unto the LORD with the harp; with the
harp, and the voice of a psalm.
6 With trumpets and sound of cornet make a joy-
ful noise before the LORD, the King.
7 Let the sea roar, and the fulness thereof; the
world, and they that dwell therein.
8 Let the floods clap *their* hands: let the hills be
joyful together
9 Before the LORD; for he cometh to judge the
earth: with righteousness shall he judge the world,
and the people with equity.

Psalm 99

1 The LORD reigneth; let the people tremble: he
sitteth *between* the cherubims; let the earth be
moved.
2 The LORD *is* great in Zion; and he *is* high above
all the people.
3 Let them praise thy great and terrible name; *for*
it *is* holy.

4 The king's strength also loveth judgment; thou
dost establish equity, thou executest judgment
and righteousness in Jacob.
5 Exalt ye the LORD our God, and worship at his
footstool; *for* he *is* holy.
6 Moses and Aaron among his priests, and Sam-
uel among them that call upon his name; they
called upon the LORD, and he answered them.
7 He spake unto them in the cloudy pillar: they kept
his testimonies, and the ordinance *that* he gave
them.
8 Thou answeredst them, O LORD our God: thou
wast a God that forgavest them, though thou
tookest vengeance of their inventions.
9 Exalt the LORD our God, and worship at his holy
hill; for the LORD our God *is* holy.

Psalm 100

A Psalm of praise.

1 Make a joyful noise unto the LORD, all ye lands.
2 Serve the LORD with gladness: come before his
presence with singing.
3 Know ye that the LORD he *is* God: *it is* he *that*
hath made us, and not we ourselves; *we are* his
people, and the sheep of his pasture.
4 Enter into his gates with thanksgiving, *and* into
his courts with praise: be thankful unto him, *and*
bless his name.

5 For the LORD *is* good; his mercy *is* everlasting;
and his truth *endureth* to all generations.

Psalm 101

A Psalm of David.

1 I will sing of mercy and judgment: unto thee,
O LORD, will I sing.
2 I will behave myself wisely in a perfect way. O
when wilt thou come unto me? I will walk within
my house with a perfect heart.
3 I will set no wicked thing before mine eyes: I
hate the work of them that turn aside; *it* shall not
cleave to me.
4 A froward heart shall depart from me: I will not
know a wicked *person*.
5 Whoso privily slandereth his neighbour, him will
I cut off: him that hath an high look and a proud
heart will not I suffer.
6 Mine eyes *shall be* upon the faithful of the land,
that they may dwell with me: he that walketh in a
perfect way, he shall serve me.
7 He that worketh deceit shall not dwell within
my house: he that telleth lies shall not tarry in my
sight.
8 I will early destroy all the wicked of the land;
that I may cut off all wicked doers from the city
of the LORD.

Psalm 102

A Prayer of the afflicted, when he is overwhelmed,
and poureth out his complaint before the LORD.

1 Hear my prayer, O LORD, and let my cry come
unto thee.
2 Hide not thy face from me in the day *when* I am
in trouble; incline thine ear unto me: in the day
when I call answer me speedily.
3 For my days are consumed like smoke, and my
bones are burned as an hearth.
4 My heart is smitten, and withered like grass; so
that I forget to eat my bread.
5 By reason of the voice of my groaning my bones
cleave to my skin.
6 I am like a pelican of the wilderness: I am like an
owl of the desert.
7 I watch, and am as a sparrow alone upon the
house top.
8 Mine enemies reproach me all the day; *and*
they that are mad against me are sworn against
me.
9 For I have eaten ashes like bread, and mingled
my drink with weeping,
10 Because of thine indignation and thy wrath:
for thou hast lifted me up, and cast me down.
11 My days *are* like a shadow that declineth; and I
am withered like grass.

12 But thou, O LORD, shall endure for ever; and
thy remembrance unto all generations.
13 Thou shalt arise, *and* have mercy upon Zion:
for the time to favour her, yea, the set time, is
come.
14 For thy servants take pleasure in her stones,
and favour the dust thereof.
15 So the heathen shall fear the name of the
LORD, and all the kings of the earth thy glory.
16 When the LORD shall build up Zion, he shall
appear in his glory.
17 He will regard the prayer of the destitute, and
not despise their prayer.
18 This shall be written for the generation to
come: and the people which shall be created shall
praise the LORD.
19 For he hath looked down from the height of
his sanctuary; from heaven did the LORD behold
the earth;
20 To hear the groaning of the prisoner; to loose
those that are appointed to death;
21 To declare the name of the LORD in Zion, and
his praise in Jerusalem;
22 When the people are gathered together, and
the kingdoms, to serve the LORD.
23 He weakened my strength in the way; he
shortened my days.

24 I said, O my God, take me not away in the
midst of my days: thy years *are* throughout all
generations.
25 Of old hast thou laid the foundation of the
earth: and the heavens *are* the work of thy
hands.
26 They shall perish, but thou shalt endure: yea,
all of them shall wax old like a garment; as a ves-
ture shalt thou change them, and they shall be
changed:
27 But thou *art* the same, and thy years shall have
no end.
28 The children of thy servants shall contin-
ue, and their seed shall be established before
thee.

Psalm 103

A Psalm *of David.*

1 Bless the LORD, O my soul: and all that is with-
in me, *bless* his holy name.
2 Bless the LORD, O my soul, and forget not all
his benefits:
3 Who forgiveth all thine iniquities; who healeth
all thy diseases;
4 Who redeemeth thy life from destruction; who
crowneth thee with lovingkindness and tender
mercies;

REST JOY GRACE RENEWAL

5 Who satisfieth thy mouth with good *things; so*
that thy youth is renewed like the eagle's.
6 The LORD executeth righteousness and judg-
ment for all that are oppressed.
7 He made known his ways unto Moses, his acts
unto the children of Israel.
8 The LORD *is* merciful and gracious, slow to
anger, and plenteous in mercy.
9 He will not always chide: neither will he keep
his anger for ever.
10 He hath not dealt with us after our sins; nor
rewarded us according to our iniquities.
11 For as the heaven is high above the earth, so
great is his mercy toward them that fear him.
12 As far as the east is from the west, *so* far hath
he removed our transgressions from us.
13 Like as a father pitieth *his* children, *so* the LORD
pitieth them that fear him.
14 For he knoweth our frame; he remembereth
that we *are* dust.
15 *As for* man, his days *are* as grass: as a flower of
the field, so he flourisheth.
16 For the wind passeth over it, and it is gone; and
the place thereof shall know it no more.
17 But the mercy of the LORD *is* from everlasting
to everlasting upon them that fear him, and his
righteousness unto children's children;

PEACE COMFORT HOPE STRENGTH GRATITUDE

18 To such as keep his covenant, and to those that
remember his commandments to do them.
19 The LORD hath prepared his throne in the
heavens; and his kingdom ruleth over all.
20 Bless the LORD, ye his angels, that excel in
strength, that do his commandments, hearken-
ing unto the voice of his word.
21 Bless ye the LORD, all *ye* his hosts; *ye* ministers
of his, that do his pleasure.
22 Bless the LORD, all his works in all places of his
dominion: bless the LORD, O my soul.

Psalm 104

1 Bless the LORD, O my soul. O LORD my God,
thou art very great; thou art clothed with honour
and majesty.
2 Who coverest *thyself* with light as *with* a garment:
who stretchest out the heavens like a curtain:
3 Who layeth the beams of his chambers in the
waters: who maketh the clouds his chariot: who
walketh upon the wings of the wind:
4 Who maketh his angels spirits; his ministers a
flaming fire:
5 *Who* laid the foundations of the earth, *that* it
should not be removed for ever.
6 Thou coveredst it with the deep as *with* a gar-
ment: the waters stood above the mountains.

7 At thy rebuke they fled; at the voice of thy
thunder they hasted away.
8 They go up by the mountains; they go down by
the valleys unto the place which thou hast found-
ed for them.
9 Thou hast set a bound that they may not pass
over; that they turn not again to cover the earth.
10 He sendeth the springs into the valleys, *which*
run among the hills.
11 They give drink to every beast of the field: the
wild asses quench their thirst.
12 By them shall the fowls of the heaven have
their habitation, *which* sing among the branches.
13 He watereth the hills from his chambers: the
earth is satisfied with the fruit of thy works.
14 He causeth the grass to grow for the cattle,
and herb for the service of man: that he may bring
forth food out of the earth;
15 And wine *that* maketh glad the heart of man,
and oil to make *his* face to shine, and bread *which*
strengtheneth man's heart.
16 The trees of the LORD are full *of sap;* the cedars
of Lebanon, which he hath planted;
17 Where the birds make their nests: *as for* the
stork, the fir trees *are* her house.
18 The high hills *are* a refuge for the wild goats;
and the rocks for the conies.

19 He appointed the moon for seasons: the sun
knoweth his going down.
20 Thou makest darkness, and it is night: where-
in all the beasts of the forest do creep *forth*.
21 The young lions roar after their prey, and seek
their meat from God.
22 The sun ariseth, they gather themselves
together, and lay them down in their dens.
23 Man goeth forth unto his work and to his
labour until the evening.
24 O LORD, how manifold are thy works! in wis-
dom hast thou made them all: the earth is full of
thy riches.
25 *So is* this great and wide sea, wherein *are* things
creeping innumerable, both small and great
beasts.
26 There go the ships: *there is* that leviathan,
whom thou hast made to play therein.
27 These wait all upon thee; that thou mayest give
them their meat in due season.
28 *That* thou givest them they gather: thou open-
est thine hand, they are filled with good.
29 Thou hidest thy face, they are troubled: thou
takest away their breath, they die, and return to
their dust.
30 Thou sendest forth thy spirit, they are creat-
ed: and thou renewest the face of the earth.

REST JOY GRACE RENEWAL

31 The glory of the LORD shall endure for ever: the
LORD shall rejoice in his works.
32 He looketh on the earth, and it trembleth: he
toucheth the hills, and they smoke.
33 I will sing unto the LORD as long as I live: I will
sing praise to my God while I have my being.
34 My meditation of him shall be sweet: I will be
glad in the LORD.
35 Let the sinners be consumed out of the earth,
and let the wicked be no more. Bless thou the
LORD, O my soul. Praise ye the LORD.

Psalm 105

1 O give thanks unto the LORD; call upon his
name: make known his deeds among the people.
2 Sing unto him, sing psalms unto him: talk ye of
all his wondrous works.
3 Glory ye in his holy name: let the heart of them
rejoice that seek the LORD.
4 Seek the LORD, and his strength: seek his face
evermore.
5 Remember his marvellous works that he hath
done; his wonders, and the judgments of his mouth;
6 O ye seed of Abraham his servant, ye children
of Jacob his chosen.
7 He *is* the LORD our God: his judgments *are* in all
the earth.

8 He hath remembered his covenant for ever, the
word *which* he commanded to a thousand gener-
ations.
9 Which *covenant* he made with Abraham, and
his oath unto Isaac;
10 And confirmed the same unto Jacob for a law,
and to Israel *for* an everlasting covenant:
11 Saying, Unto thee will I give the land of Canaan,
the lot of your inheritance:
12 When they were *but* a few men in number; yea,
very few, and strangers in it.
13 When they went from one nation to another,
from *one* kingdom to another people;
14 He suffered no man to do them wrong: yea, he
reproved kings for their sakes;
15 *Saying,* Touch not mine anointed, and do my
prophets no harm.
16 Moreover he called for a famine upon the land:
he brake the whole staff of bread.
17 He sent a man before them, *even* Joseph, *who*
was sold for a servant:
18 Whose feet they hurt with fetters: he was laid
in iron:
19 Until the time that his word came: the word of
the LORD tried him.
20 The king sent and loosed him; *even* the ruler of
the people, and let him go free.

21 He made him lord of his house, and ruler of all
his substance:
22 To bind his princes at his pleasure; and teach
his senators wisdom.
23 Israel also came into Egypt; and Jacob
sojourned in the land of Ham.
24 And he increased his people greatly; and made
them stronger than their enemies.
25 He turned their heart to hate his people, to
deal subtilly with his servants.
26 He sent Moses his servant; *and* Aaron whom
he had chosen.
27 They shewed his signs among them, and won-
ders in the land of Ham.
28 He sent darkness, and made it dark; and they
rebelled not against his word.
29 He turned their waters into blood, and slew
their fish.
30 Their land brought forth frogs in abundance,
in the chambers of their kings.
31 He spake, and there came divers sorts of flies,
and lice in all their coasts.
32 He gave them hail for rain, *and* flaming fire in
their land.
33 He smote their vines also and their fig trees;
and brake the trees of their coasts.
34 He spake, and the locusts came, and caterpil-
lers, and that without number,

35 And did eat up all the herbs in their land, and
devoured the fruit of their ground.
36 He smote also all the firstborn in their land,
the chief of all their strength.
37 He brought them forth also with silver and
gold: and *there was* not one feeble *person* among
their tribes.
38 Egypt was glad when they departed: for the
fear of them fell upon them.
39 He spread a cloud for a covering; and fire to
give light in the night.
40 *The people* asked, and he brought quails, and
satisfied them with the bread of heaven.
41 He opened the rock, and the waters gushed
out; they ran in the dry places *like* a river.
42 For he remembered his holy promise, *and*
Abraham his servant.
43 And he brought forth his people with joy, *and*
his chosen with gladness:
44 And gave them the lands of the heathen: and
they inherited the labour of the people;
45 That they might observe his statutes, and keep
his laws. Praise ye the LORD.

Psalm 106

1 Praise ye the LORD. O give thanks unto the
LORD; for *he is* good: for his mercy *endureth* for
ever.

2 Who can utter the mighty acts of the LORD?
who can shew forth all his praise?
3 Blessed *are* they that keep judgment, *and* he
that doeth righteousness at all times.
4 Remember me, O LORD, with the favour *that*
thou bearest unto thy people: O visit me with thy
salvation;
5 That I may see the good of thy chosen, that I
may rejoice in the gladness of thy nation, that I
may glory with thine inheritance.
6 We have sinned with our fathers, we have com-
mitted iniquity, we have done wickedly.
7 Our fathers understood not thy wonders in
Egypt; they remembered not the multitude of
thy mercies; but provoked *him* at the sea, *even* at
the Red sea.
8 Nevertheless he saved them for his name's
sake, that he might make his mighty power to be
known.
9 He rebuked the Red sea also, and it was dried
up: so he led them through the depths, as through
the wilderness.
10 And he saved them from the hand of him that
hated *them*, and redeemed them from the hand
of the enemy.
11 And the waters covered their enemies: there
was not one of them left.

12 Then believed they his words; they sang his praise.
13 They soon forgat his works; they waited not for
his counsel:
14 But lusted exceedingly in the wilderness, and
tempted God in the desert.
15 And he gave them their request; but sent lean-
ness into their soul.
16 They envied Moses also in the camp, *and* Aaron
the saint of the LORD.
17 The earth opened and swallowed up Dathan
and covered the company of Abiram.
18 And a fire was kindled in their company; the
flame burned up the wicked.
19 They made a calf in Horeb, and worshipped the
molten image.
20 Thus they changed their glory into the simili-
tude of an ox that eateth grass.
21 They forgat God their saviour, which had done
great things in Egypt;
22 Wondrous works in the land of Ham, *and* ter-
rible things by the Red sea.
23 Therefore he said that he would destroy them,
had not Moses his chosen stood before him in the
breach, to turn away his wrath, lest he should
destroy *them.*
24 Yea, they despised the pleasant land, they
believed not his word:

25 But murmured in their tents, *and* hearkened
not unto the voice of the LORD.
26 Therefore he lifted up his hand against them,
to overthrow them in the wilderness:
27 To overthrow their seed also among the nations,
and to scatter them in the lands.
28 They joined themselves also unto Baal-peor,
and ate the sacrifices of the dead.
29 Thus they provoked *him* to anger with their
inventions: and the plague brake in upon
them.
30 Then stood up Phinehas, and executed judg-
ment: and *so* the plague was stayed.
31 And that was counted unto him for righteous-
ness unto all generations for evermore.
32 They angered *him* also at the waters of strife,
so that it went ill with Moses for their sakes:
33 Because they provoked his spirit, so that he
spake unadvisedly with his lips.
34 They did not destroy the nations, concerning
whom the LORD commanded them:
35 But were mingled among the heathen, and
learned their works.
36 And they served their idols: which were a snare
unto them.
37 Yea, they sacrificed their sons and their daugh-
ters unto devils,

38 And shed innocent blood, *even* the blood of
their sons and of their daughters, whom they sac-
rificed unto the idols of Canaan: and the land was
polluted with blood.
39 Thus were they defiled with their own works,
and went a whoring with their own inventions.
40 Therefore was the wrath of the LORD kindled
against his people, insomuch that he abhorred his
own inheritance.
41 And he gave them into the hand of the hea-
then; and they that hated them ruled over
them.
42 Their enemies also oppressed them, and they
were brought into subjection under their hand.
43 Many times did he deliver them; but they pro-
voked *him* with their counsel, and were brought
low for their iniquity.
44 Nevertheless he regarded their affliction,
when he heard their cry:
45 And he remembered for them his covenant,
and repented according to the multitude of his
mercies.
46 He made them also to be pitied of all those
that carried them captives.
47 Save us, O LORD our God, and gather us from
among the heathen, to give thanks unto thy holy
name, *and* to triumph in thy praise.

48 Blessed *be* the LORD God of Israel from ever-
lasting to everlasting: and let all the people say,
Amen. Praise ye the LORD.

BOOK 5

Psalm 107

1 O give thanks unto the LORD, for *he is* good: for
his mercy *endureth* for ever.
2 Let the redeemed of the LORD say so, whom he
hath redeemed from the hand of the enemy;
3 And gathered them out of the lands, from the
east, and from the west, from the north, and from
the south.
4 They wandered in the wilderness in a solitary
way; they found no city to dwell in.
5 Hungry and thirsty, their soul fainted in them.
6 Then they cried unto the LORD in their trouble,
and he delivered them out of their distresses.
7 And he led them forth by the right way, that
they might go to a city of habitation.
8 Oh that *men* would praise the LORD *for* his
goodness, and *for* his wonderful works to the chil-
dren of men!
9 For he satisfieth the longing soul, and filleth the
hungry soul with goodness.

10 Such as sit in darkness and in the shadow of
death, *being* bound in affliction and iron;
11 Because they rebelled against the words of
God, and contemned the counsel of the most
High:
12 Therefore he brought down their heart with
labour; they fell down, and *there was* none to help.
13 Then they cried unto the LORD in their trou-
ble, *and* he saved them out of their distresses.
14 He brought them out of darkness and the
shadow of death, and brake their bands in sunder.
15 Oh that *men* would praise the LORD *for* his
goodness, and *for* his wonderful works to the chil-
dren of men!
16 For he hath broken the gates of brass, and cut
the bars of iron in sunder.
17 Fools because of their transgression, and
because of their iniquities, are afflicted.
18 Their soul abhorreth all manner of meat; and
they draw near unto the gates of death.
19 Then they cry unto the LORD in their trouble,
and he saveth them out of their distresses.
20 He sent his word, and healed them, and deliv-
ered *them* from their destructions.
21 Oh that *men* would praise the LORD *for* his
goodness, and *for* his wonderful works to the chil-
dren of men!

22 And let them sacrifice the sacrifices of
thanksgiving, and declare his works with rejoic-
ing.
23 They that go down to the sea in ships, that do
business in great waters;
24 These see the works of the LORD, and his won-
ders in the deep.
25 For he commandeth, and raiseth the stormy
wind, which lifteth up the waves thereof.
26 They mount up to the heaven, they go down
again to the depths: their soul is melted because
of trouble.
27 They reel to and fro, and stagger like a drunk-
en man, and are at their wit's end.
28 Then they cry unto the LORD in their trouble,
and he bringeth them out of their distresses.
29 He maketh the storm a calm, so that the waves
thereof are still.
30 Then are they glad because they be quiet; so
he bringeth them unto their desired haven.
31 Oh that *men* would praise the LORD *for* his
goodness, and *for* his wonderful works to the chil-
dren of men!
32 Let them exalt him also in the congregation of
the people, and praise him in the assembly of the
elders.
33 He turneth rivers into a wilderness, and the
watersprings into dry ground;

34 A fruitful land into barrenness, for the wick-
edness of them that dwell therein.
35 He turneth the wilderness into a standing
water, and dry ground into watersprings.
36 And there he maketh the hungry to dwell, that
they may prepare a city for habitation;
37 And sow the fields, and plant vineyards, which
may yield fruits of increase.
38 He blesseth them also, so that they are multi-
plied greatly; and suffereth not their cattle to
decrease.
39 Again, they are minished and brought low
through oppression, affliction, and sorrow.
40 He poureth contempt upon princes, and
causeth them to wander in the wilderness, *where
there is* no way.
41 Yet setteth he the poor on high from affliction,
and maketh *him* families like a flock.
42 The righteous shall see *it*, and rejoice: and all
iniquity shall stop her mouth.
43 Whoso *is* wise, and will observe these *things*,
even they shall understand the lovingkindness of
the LORD.

Psalm 108

A Song or Psalm of David.

1 O God, my heart is fixed; I will sing and give
praise, even with my glory.

2 Awake, psaltery and harp: I *myself* will awake
early.
3 I will praise thee, O LORD, among the people:
and I will sing praises unto thee among the
nations.
4 For thy mercy *is* great above the heavens: and
thy truth *reacheth* unto the clouds.
5 Be thou exalted, O God, above the heavens:
and thy glory above all the earth;
6 That thy beloved may be delivered: save *with*
thy right hand, and answer me.
7 God hath spoken in his holiness; I will rejoice, I
will divide Shechem, and mete out the valley of
Succoth.
8 Gilead *is* mine; Manasseh *is* mine; Ephraim
also *is* the strength of mine head; Judah *is* my
lawgiver;
9 Moab *is* my washpot; over Edom will I cast out
my shoe; over Philistia will I triumph.
10 Who will bring me into the strong city? who
will lead me into Edom?
11 *Wilt* not *thou,* O God, *who* hast cast us off?
and wilt not thou, O God, go forth with our
hosts?
12 Give us help from trouble: for vain *is* the help
of man.
13 Through God we shall do valiantly: for he *it is*
that shall tread down our enemies.

Psalm 109

To the chief Musician, A Psalm of David.

1 Hold not thy peace, O God of my praise;
2 For the mouth of the wicked and the mouth of
the deceitful are opened against me: they have
spoken against me with a lying tongue.
3 They compassed me about also with words of
hatred; and fought against me without a cause.
4 For my love they are my adversaries: but I *give*
myself unto prayer.
5 And they have rewarded me evil for good, and
hatred for my love.
6 Set thou a wicked man over him: and let Satan
stand at his right hand.
7 When he shall be judged, let him be con-
demned: and let his prayer become sin.
8 Let his days be few; *and* let another take his
office.
9 Let his children be fatherless, and his wife a
widow.
10 Let his children be continually vagabonds,
and beg: let them seek *their bread* also out of
their desolate places.
11 Let the extortioner catch all that he hath; and
let the strangers spoil his labour.
12 Let there be none to extend mercy unto him:
neither let there be any to favour his fatherless
children.

13 Let his posterity be cut off; *and* in the generation following let their name be blotted out.
14 Let the iniquity of his fathers be remembered with the LORD; and let not the sin of his mother be blotted out.
15 Let them be before the LORD continually, that he may cut off the memory of them from the earth.
16 Because that he remembered not to shew mercy, but persecuted the poor and needy man, that he might even slay the broken in heart.
17 As he loved cursing, so let it come unto him: as he delighted not in blessing, so let it be far from him.
18 As he clothed himself with cursing like as with his garment, so let it come into his bowels like water, and like oil into his bones.
19 Let it be unto him as the garment *which* covereth him, and for a girdle wherewith he is girded continually.
20 *Let* this *be* the reward of mine adversaries from the LORD, and of them that speak evil against my soul.
21 But do thou for me, O GOD the Lord, for thy name's sake: because thy mercy *is* good, deliver thou me.
22 For I *am* poor and needy, and my heart is wounded within me.

23 I am gone like the shadow when it declineth: I
am tossed up and down as the locust.
24 My knees are weak through fasting; and my
flesh faileth of fatness.
25 I became also a reproach unto them: *when* they
looked upon me they shaked their heads.
26 Help me, O LORD my God: O save me accord-
ing to thy mercy:
27 That they may know that this *is* thy hand; *that*
thou, LORD, hast done it.
28 Let them curse, but bless thou: when they
arise, let them be ashamed; but let thy servant
rejoice.
29 Let mine adversaries be clothed with shame,
and let them cover themselves with their own
confusion, as with a mantle.
30 I will greatly praise the LORD with my mouth;
yea, I will praise him among the multitude.
31 For he shall stand at the right hand of the poor,
to save *him* from those that condemn his soul.

Psalm 110

A Psalm of David.

1 The LORD said unto my Lord, Sit thou at my
right hand, until I make thine enemies thy foot-
stool.
2 The LORD shall send the rod of thy strength out
of Zion: rule thou in the midst of thine enemies.

3 Thy people *shall be* willing in the day of thy
power, in the beauties of holiness from the
womb of the morning: thou hast the dew of thy
youth.
4 The LORD hath sworn, and will not repent, Thou
art a priest for ever after the order of Melchize-
dek.
5 The Lord at thy right hand shall strike through
kings in the day of his wrath.
6 He shall judge among the heathen, he shall fill
the places with the dead bodies; he shall wound the
heads over many countries.
7 He shall drink of the brook in the way: there-
fore shall he lift up the head.

Psalm 111

1 Praise ye the LORD. I will praise the LORD with
my whole heart, in the assembly of the upright,
and *in* the congregation.
2 The works of the LORD *are* great, sought out of
all them that have pleasure therein.
3 His work *is* honourable and glorious: and his
righteousness endureth for ever.
4 He hath made his wonderful works to be
remembered: the LORD *is* gracious and full of
compassion.
5 He hath given meat unto them that fear him:
he will ever be mindful of his covenant.

6 He hath shewed his people the power of his
works, that he may give them the heritage of the
heathen.
7 The works of his hands *are* verity and judgment;
all his commandments *are* sure.
8 They stand fast for ever and ever, *and are* done
in truth and uprightness.
9 He sent redemption unto his people: he hath
commanded his covenant for ever: holy and rev-
erend *is* his name.
10 The fear of the LORD *is* the beginning of wis-
dom: a good understanding have all they that
do *his commandments:* his praise endureth for
ever.

Psalm 112

1 Praise ye the LORD. Blessed *is* the man *that*
feareth the LORD, *that* delighteth greatly in his
commandments.
2 His seed shall be mighty upon earth: the gen-
eration of the upright shall be blessed.
3 Wealth and riches *shall be* in his house: and his
righteousness endureth for ever.
4 Unto the upright there ariseth light in the dark-
ness: *he is* gracious, and full of compassion, and
righteous.
5 A good man sheweth favour, and lendeth: he
will guide his affairs with discretion.

REST JOY GRACE RENEWAL

6 Surely he shall not be moved for ever: the righ-
teous shall be in everlasting remembrance.
7 He shall not be afraid of evil tidings: his heart is
fixed, trusting in the LORD.
8 His heart *is* established, he shall not be afraid,
until he see *his desire* upon his enemies.
9 He hath dispersed, he hath given to the poor;
his righteousness endureth for ever; his horn shall
be exalted with honour.
10 The wicked shall see *it*, and be grieved; he shall
gnash with his teeth, and melt away: the desire of
the wicked shall perish.

Psalm 113

1 Praise ye the LORD. Praise, O ye servants of the
LORD, praise the name of the LORD.
2 Blessed be the name of the LORD from this time
forth and for evermore.
3 From the rising of the sun unto the going down
of the same the LORD'S name *is* to be praised.
4 The LORD *is* high above all nations, *and* his glory
above the heavens.
5 Who *is* like unto the LORD our God, who dwell-
eth on high,
6 Who humbleth *himself* to behold *the things that*
are in heaven, and in the earth!
7 He raiseth up the poor out of the dust, *and*
lifteth the needy out of the dunghill;

8 That he may set *him* with princes, *even* with the
princes of his people.
9 He maketh the barren woman to keep house, *and*
to be a joyful mother of children. Praise ye the LORD.

Psalm 114

1 When Israel went out of Egypt, the house of
Jacob from a people of strange language;
2 Judah was his sanctuary, *and* Israel his domin-
ion.
3 The sea saw *it*, and fled: Jordan was driven back.
4 The mountains skipped like rams, *and* the little
hills like lambs.
5 What *ailed* thee, O thou sea, that thou fled-
dest? thou Jordan, *that* thou wast driven back?
6 Ye mountains, *that* ye skipped like rams; *and* ye
little hills, like lambs?
7 Tremble, thou earth, at the presence of the
Lord, at the presence of the God of Jacob;
8 Which turned the rock *into* a standing water,
the flint into a fountain of waters.

Psalm 115

1 Not unto us, O LORD, not unto us, but unto thy
name give glory, for thy mercy, *and* for thy truth's
sake.
2 Wherefore should the heathen say, Where *is*
now their God?

3 But our God *is* in the heavens: he hath done
whatsoever he hath pleased.
4 Their idols *are* silver and gold, the work of men's
hands.
5 They have mouths, but they speak not: eyes
have they, but they see not:
6 They have ears, but they hear not: noses have
they, but they smell not:
7 They have hands, but they handle not: feet have
they, but they walk not: neither speak they
through their throat.
8 They that make them are like unto them; *so is*
every one that trusteth in them.
9 O Israel, trust thou in the LORD: he *is* their help
and their shield.
10 O house of Aaron, trust in the LORD: he *is* their
help and their shield.
11 Ye that fear the LORD, trust in the LORD: he *is*
their help and their shield.
12 The LORD hath been mindful of us: he will bless
us; he will bless the house of Israel; he will bless
the house of Aaron.
13 He will bless them that fear the LORD, *both*
small and great.
14 The LORD shall increase you more and more,
you and your children.
15 Ye *are* blessed of the LORD which made heav-
en and earth.

16 The heaven, *even* the heavens, *are* the LORD'S:
but the earth hath he given to the children of
men.
17 The dead praise not the LORD, neither any that
go down into silence.
18 But we will bless the LORD from this time forth
and for evermore. Praise the LORD.

Psalm 116

1 I love the LORD, because he hath heard my voice
and my supplications.
2 Because he hath inclined his ear unto me,
therefore will I call upon *him* as long as I live.
3 The sorrows of death compassed me, and the
pains of hell gat hold upon me: I found trouble and
sorrow.
4 Then called I upon the name of the LORD; O
LORD, I beseech thee, deliver my soul.
5 Gracious *is* the LORD, and righteous; yea, our
God *is* merciful.
6 The LORD preserveth the simple: I was brought
low, and he helped me.
7 Return unto thy rest, O my soul; for the LORD
hath dealt bountifully with thee.
8 For thou hast delivered my soul from death,
mine eyes from tears, *and* my feet from falling.
9 I will walk before the LORD in the land of the liv-
ing.

REST JOY GRACE RENEWAL

10 I believed, therefore have I spoken; I was greatly afflicted:

11 I said in my haste, All men *are* liars.

12 What shall I render unto the LORD *for* all his benefits toward me?

13 I will take the cup of salvation, and call upon the name of the LORD.

14 I will pay my vows unto the LORD now in the presence of all his people.

15 Precious in the sight of the LORD *is* the death of his saints.

16 O LORD, truly I *am* thy servant; I *am* thy servant, *and* the son of thine handmaid: thou hast loosed my bonds.

17 I will offer to thee the sacrifice of thanksgiving, and will call upon the name of the LORD.

18 I will pay my vows unto the LORD now in the presence of all his people.

19 In the courts of the LORD'S house, in the midst of thee, O Jerusalem. Praise ye the LORD.

Psalm 117

1 O praise the LORD, all ye nations: praise him, all ye people.

2 For his merciful kindness is great toward us: and the truth of the LORD *endureth* for ever. Praise ye the LORD.

PEACE | COMFORT | HOPE | STRENGTH | GRATITUDE

Psalm 118

1 O give thanks unto the LORD; for *he is* good:
because his mercy *endureth* for ever.
2 Let Israel now say, that his mercy *endureth* for ever.
3 Let the house of Aaron now say, that his mercy
endureth for ever.
4 Let them now that fear the LORD say, that his
mercy *endureth* for ever.
5 I called upon the LORD in distress: the LORD
answered me, *and set me* in a large place.
6 The LORD *is* on my side; I will not fear: what can
man do unto me?
7 The LORD taketh my part with them that help
me: therefore shall I see *my desire* upon them that
hate me.
8 *It is* better to trust in the LORD than to put con-
fidence in man.
9 *It is* better to trust in the LORD than to put con-
fidence in princes.
10 All nations compassed me about: but in the
name of the LORD will I destroy them.
11 They compassed me about; yea, they com-
passed me about: but in the name of the LORD I
will destroy them.
12 They compassed me about like bees; they are
quenched as the fire of thorns: for in the name of
the LORD I will destroy them.

REST JOY GRACE RENEWAL

13 Thou hast thrust sore at me that I might fall:
but the LORD helped me.
14 The LORD *is* my strength and song, and is
become my salvation.
15 The voice of rejoicing and salvation *is* in the
tabernacles of the righteous: the right hand of the
LORD doeth valiantly.
16 The right hand of the LORD is exalted: the right
hand of the LORD doeth valiantly.
17 I shall not die, but live, and declare the works
of the LORD.
18 The LORD hath chastened me sore: but he hath
not given me over unto death.
19 Open to me the gates of righteousness: I will
go into them, *and* I will praise the LORD:
20 This gate of the LORD, into which the righteous
shall enter.
21 I will praise thee: for thou hast heard me, and
art become my salvation.
22 The stone *which* the builders refused is become
the head *stone* of the corner.
23 This is the LORD'S doing; it *is* marvellous in our
eyes.
24 This *is* the day *which* the LORD hath made; we
will rejoice and be glad in it.
25 Save now, I beseech thee, O LORD: O LORD, I
beseech thee, send now prosperity.

26 Blessed *be* he that cometh in the name of the
LORD: we have blessed you out of the house of the
LORD.
27 God *is* the LORD, which hath shewed us light:
bind the sacrifice with cords, *even* unto the horns
of the altar.
28 Thou *art* my God, and I will praise thee: *thou*
art my God, I will exalt thee.
29 O give thanks unto the LORD; for *he is* good:
for his mercy *endureth* for ever.

Psalm 119

ALEPH

1 Blessed *are* the undefiled in the way, who walk
in the law of the LORD.
2 Blessed *are* they that keep his testimonies, *and*
that seek him with the whole heart.
3 They also do no iniquity: they walk in his ways.
4 Thou hast commanded *us* to keep thy precepts
diligently.
5 O that my ways were directed to keep thy stat-
utes!
6 Then shall I not be ashamed, when I have
respect unto all thy commandments.
7 I will praise thee with uprightness of heart,
when I shall have learned thy righteous judg-
ments.

8 I will keep thy statutes: O forsake me not
utterly.

BETH

9 Wherewithal shall a young man cleanse his way?
by taking heed *thereto* according to thy word.
10 With my whole heart have I sought thee: O
let me not wander from thy commandments.
11 Thy word have I hid in mine heart, that I might
not sin against thee.
12 Blessed *art* thou, O LORD: teach me thy stat-
utes.
13 With my lips have I declared all the judgments
of thy mouth.
14 I have rejoiced in the way of thy testimonies,
as *much as* in all riches.
15 I will meditate in thy precepts, and have
respect unto thy ways.
16 I will delight myself in thy statutes: I will not
forget thy word.

GIMEL

17 Deal bountifully with thy servant, *that* I may
live, and keep thy word.
18 Open thou mine eyes, that I may behold won-
drous things out of thy law.
19 I *am* a stranger in the earth: hide not thy com-
mandments from me.

PEACE | COMFORT | HOPE | STRENGTH | GRATITUDE

20 My soul breaketh for the longing *that it hath*
unto thy judgments at all times.
21 Thou hast rebuked the proud *that are* cursed,
which do err from thy commandments.
22 Remove from me reproach and contempt; for
I have kept thy testimonies.
23 Princes also did sit *and* speak against me: *but*
thy servant did meditate in thy statutes.
24 Thy testimonies also *are* my delight *and* my
counsellors.

DALETH

25 My soul cleaveth unto the dust: quicken thou
me according to thy word.
26 I have declared my ways, and thou heardest
me: teach me thy statutes.
27 Make me to understand the way of thy pre-
cepts: so shall I talk of thy wondrous works.
28 My soul melteth for heaviness: strengthen
thou me according unto thy word.
29 Remove from me the way of lying: and grant
me thy law graciously.
30 I have chosen the way of truth: thy judgments
have I laid *before me*.
31 I have stuck unto thy testimonies: O LORD, put
me not to shame.
32 I will run the way of thy commandments, when
thou shalt enlarge my heart.

REST JOY GRACE RENEWAL

HE

33 Teach me, O LORD, the way of thy statutes;
and I shall keep it *unto* the end.
34 Give me understanding, and I shall keep thy
law; yea, I shall observe it with *my* whole heart.
35 Make me to go in the path of thy command-
ments; for therein do I delight.
36 Incline my heart unto thy testimonies, and not
to covetousness.
37 Turn away mine eyes from beholding vanity;
and quicken thou me in thy way.
38 Stablish thy word unto thy servant, who *is*
devoted to thy fear.
39 Turn away my reproach which I fear: for thy
judgments *are* good.
40 Behold, I have longed after thy precepts:
quicken me in thy righteousness.

VAU

41 Let thy mercies come also unto me, O LORD,
even thy salvation, according to thy word.
42 So shall I have wherewith to answer him that
reproacheth me: for I trust in thy word.
43 And take not the word of truth utterly out of
my mouth; for I have hoped in thy judgments.
44 So shall I keep thy law continually for ever and
ever.
45 And I will walk at liberty: for I seek thy precepts.

46 I will speak of thy testimonies also before
kings, and will not be ashamed.
47 And I will delight myself in thy command-
ments, which I have loved.
48 My hands also will I lift up unto thy command-
ments, which I have loved; and I will meditate in
thy statutes.

ZAIN

49 Remember the word unto thy servant, upon
which thou hast caused me to hope.
50 This *is* my comfort in my affliction: for thy
word hath quickened me.
51 The proud have had me greatly in derision: *yet*
have I not declined from thy law.
52 I remembered thy judgments of old, O LORD;
and have comforted myself.
53 Horror hath taken hold upon me because of
the wicked that forsake thy law.
54 Thy statutes have been my songs in the house
of my pilgrimage.
55 I have remembered thy name, O LORD, in the
night, and have kept thy law.
56 This I had, because I kept thy precepts.

CHETH

57 *Thou art* my portion, O LORD: I have said that
I would keep thy words.

58 I intreated thy favour with *my* whole heart: be
merciful unto me according to thy word.
59 I thought on my ways, and turned my feet
unto thy testimonies.
60 I made haste, and delayed not to keep thy
commandments.
61 The bands of the wicked have robbed me: *but*
I have not forgotten thy law.
62 At midnight I will rise to give thanks unto thee
because of thy righteous judgments.
63 I *am* a companion of all *them* that fear thee,
and of them that keep thy precepts.
64 The earth, O LORD, is full of thy mercy: teach
me thy statutes.

TETH

65 Thou hast dealt well with thy servant, O LORD,
according unto thy word.
66 Teach me good judgment and knowledge: for
I have believed thy commandments.
67 Before I was afflicted I went astray: but now
have I kept thy word.
68 Thou *art* good, and doest good; teach me thy
statutes.
69 The proud have forged a lie against me: *but* I
will keep thy precepts with *my* whole heart.
70 Their heart is as fat as grease; *but* I delight in
thy law.

71 *It is* good for me that I have been afflicted; that
I might learn thy statutes.
72 The law of thy mouth *is* better unto me than
thousands of gold and silver.

JOD

73 Thy hands have made me and fashioned me:
give me understanding, that I may learn thy
commandments.
74 They that fear thee will be glad when they see
me; because I have hoped in thy word.
75 I know, O LORD, that thy judgments *are* right,
and that *thou* in faithfulness hast afflicted me.
76 Let, I pray thee, thy merciful kindness be for my
comfort, according to thy word unto thy servant.
77 Let thy tender mercies come unto me, that I
may live: for thy law *is* my delight.
78 Let the proud be ashamed; for they dealt per-
versely with me without a cause: *but* I will medi-
tate in thy precepts.
79 Let those that fear thee turn unto me, and
those that have known thy testimonies.
80 Let my heart be sound in thy statutes; that I
be not ashamed.

CAPH

81 My soul fainteth for thy salvation: *but* I hope
in thy word.

REST JOY GRACE RENEWAL

82 Mine eyes fail for thy word, saying, When wilt
thou comfort me?
83 For I am become like a bottle in the smoke; *yet*
do I not forget thy statutes.
84 How many *are* the days of thy servant? when
wilt thou execute judgment on them that perse-
cute me?
85 The proud have digged pits for me, which *are*
not after thy law.
86 All thy commandments *are* faithful: they per-
secute me wrongfully; help thou me.
87 They had almost consumed me upon earth;
but I forsook not thy precepts.
88 Quicken me after thy lovingkindness; so shall
I keep the testimony of thy mouth.

LAMED

89 For ever, O LORD, thy word is settled in heaven.
90 Thy faithfulness *is* unto all generations: thou
hast established the earth, and it abideth.
91 They continue this day according to thine ordi-
nances: for all *are* thy servants.
92 Unless thy law *had been* my delights, I should
then have perished in mine affliction.
93 I will never forget thy precepts: for with them
thou hast quickened me.
94 I *am* thine, save me; for I have sought thy pre-
cepts.

95 The wicked have waited for me to destroy me:
but I will consider thy testimonies.
96 I have seen an end of all perfection: *but* thy
commandment *is* exceeding broad.

MEM

97 O how I love thy law! it *is* my meditation all the
day.
98 Thou through thy commandments hast made me
wiser than mine enemies: for they *are* ever with me.
99 I have more understanding than all my teach-
ers: for thy testimonies *are* my meditation.
100 I understand more than the ancients, because
I keep thy precepts.
101 I have refrained my feet from every evil way,
that I might keep thy word.
102 I have not departed from thy judgments: for
thou hast taught me.
103 How sweet are thy words unto my taste! *yea,*
sweeter than honey to my mouth!
104 Through thy precepts I get understanding:
therefore I hate every false way.

NUN

105 Thy word *is* a lamp unto my feet, and a light
unto my path.
106 I have sworn, and I will perform *it*, that I will
keep thy righteous judgments.

107 I am afflicted very much: quicken me, O
LORD, according unto thy word.
108 Accept, I beseech thee, the freewill offerings
of my mouth, O LORD, and teach me thy judg-
ments.
109 My soul *is* continually in my hand: yet do I not
forget thy law.
110 The wicked have laid a snare for me: yet I erred
not from thy precepts.
111 Thy testimonies have I taken as an heritage for
ever: for they *are* the rejoicing of my heart.
112 I have inclined mine heart to perform thy stat-
utes alway, *even unto* the end.

SAMECH

113 I hate *vain* thoughts: but thy law do I love.
114 Thou *art* my hiding place and my shield: I hope
in thy word.
115 Depart from me, ye evildoers: for I will keep
the commandments of my God.
116 Uphold me according unto thy word, that I
may live: and let me not be ashamed of my hope.
117 Hold thou me up, and I shall be safe: and I will
have respect unto thy statutes continually.
118 Thou hast trodden down all them that err from
thy statutes: for their deceit *is* falsehood.
119 Thou puttest away all the wicked of the earth
like dross: therefore I love thy testimonies.

120 My flesh trembleth for fear of thee; and I am
afraid of thy judgments.

AIN

121 I have done judgment and justice: leave me
not to mine oppressors.
122 Be surety for thy servant for good: let not the
proud oppress me.
123 Mine eyes fail for thy salvation, and for the
word of thy righteousness.
124 Deal with thy servant according unto thy
mercy, and teach me thy statutes.
125 I *am* thy servant; give me understanding, that
I may know thy testimonies.
126 *It is* time for *thee,* LORD, to work: *for* they have
made void thy law.
127 Therefore I love thy commandments above
gold; yea, above fine gold.
128 Therefore I esteem all *thy* precepts *concern-*
ing all *things to be* right; *and* I hate every false way.

PE

129 Thy testimonies *are* wonderful: therefore
doth my soul keep them.
130 The entrance of thy words giveth light; it
giveth understanding unto the simple.
131 I opened my mouth, and panted: for I longed
for thy commandments.

REST JOY GRACE RENEWAL

132 Look thou upon me, and be merciful unto
me, as thou usest to do unto those that love thy
name.
133 Order my steps in thy word: and let not any
iniquity have dominion over me.
134 Deliver me from the oppression of man: so
will I keep thy precepts.
135 Make thy face to shine upon thy servant; and
teach me thy statutes.
136 Rivers of waters run down mine eyes, because
they keep not thy law.

TZADDI

137 Righteous *art* thou, O LORD, and upright *are*
thy judgments.
138 Thy testimonies *that* thou hast commanded
are righteous and very faithful.
139 My zeal hath consumed me, because mine
enemies have forgotten thy words.
140 Thy word *is* very pure: therefore thy servant
loveth it.
141 I *am* small and despised: *yet* do not I forget thy
precepts.
142 Thy righteousness *is* an everlasting righteous-
ness, and thy law *is* the truth.
143 Trouble and anguish have taken hold on me:
yet thy commandments *are* my delights.

144 The righteousness of thy testimonies *is* ever-
lasting: give me understanding, and I shall live.

KOPH

145 I cried with *my* whole heart; hear me, O LORD:
I will keep thy statutes.
146 I cried unto thee; save me, and I shall keep thy
testimonies.
147 I prevented the dawning of the morning, and
cried: I hoped in thy word.
148 Mine eyes prevent the *night* watches, that I
might meditate in thy word.
149 Hear my voice according unto thy loving-
kindness: O LORD, quicken me according to thy
judgment.
150 They draw nigh that follow after mischief:
they are far from thy law.
151 Thou *art* near, O LORD; and all thy command-
ments *are* truth.
152 Concerning thy testimonies, I have known of
old that thou hast founded them for ever.

RESH

153 Consider mine affliction, and deliver me: for
I do not forget thy law.
154 Plead my cause, and deliver me: quicken me
according to thy word.

REST JOY GRACE RENEWAL

155 Salvation *is* far from the wicked: for they seek
not thy statutes.
156 Great *are* thy tender mercies, O LORD: quick-
en me according to thy judgments.
157 Many *are* my persecutors and mine enemies;
yet do I not decline from thy testimonies.
158 I beheld the transgressors, and was grieved;
because they kept not thy word.
159 Consider how I love thy precepts: quicken
me, O LORD, according to thy lovingkindness.
160 Thy word *is* true *from* the beginning: and every
one of thy righteous judgments *endureth* for ever.

SCHIN

161 Princes have persecuted me without a cause:
but my heart standeth in awe of thy word.
162 I rejoice at thy word, as one that findeth great
spoil.
163 I hate and abhor lying: *but* thy law do I love.
164 Seven times a day do I praise thee because of
thy righteous judgments.
165 Great peace have they which love thy law: and
nothing shall offend them.
166 LORD, I have hoped for thy salvation, and done
thy commandments.
167 My soul hath kept thy testimonies; and I love
them exceedingly.

168 I have kept thy precepts and thy testimonies:
for all my ways *are* before thee.

TAU

169 Let my cry come near before thee, O LORD:
give me understanding according to thy word.
170 Let my supplication come before thee: deliv-
er me according to thy word.
171 My lips shall utter praise, when thou hast
taught me thy statutes.
172 My tongue shall speak of thy word: for all thy
commandments *are* righteousness.
173 Let thine hand help me; for I have chosen thy
precepts.
174 I have longed for thy salvation, O LORD; and
thy law *is* my delight.
175 Let my soul live, and it shall praise thee; and
let thy judgments help me.
176 I have gone astray like a lost sheep; seek thy
servant; for I do not forget thy commandments.

Psalm 120

A Song of degrees.

1 In my distress I cried unto the LORD, and he
heard me.
2 Deliver my soul, O LORD, from lying lips, *and*
from a deceitful tongue.

3 What shall be given unto thee? or what shall be
done unto thee, thou false tongue?
4 Sharp arrows of the mighty, with coals of juniper.
5 Woe is me, that I sojourn in Mesech, *that* I dwell
in the tents of Kedar!
6 My soul hath long dwelt with him that hateth
peace.
7 I *am for* peace: but when I speak, they *are* for war.

Psalm 121

A Song of degrees.

1 I will lift up mine eyes unto the hills, from
whence cometh my help.
2 My help *cometh* from the LORD, which made
heaven and earth.
3 He will not suffer thy foot to be moved: he that
keepeth thee will not slumber.
4 Behold, he that keepeth Israel shall neither
slumber nor sleep.
5 The LORD *is* thy keeper: the LORD *is* thy shade
upon thy right hand.
6 The sun shall not smite thee by day, nor the
moon by night.
7 The LORD shall preserve thee from all evil: he
shall preserve thy soul.
8 The LORD shall preserve thy going out and thy
coming in from this time forth, and even for ever-
more.

PEACE COMFORT HOPE STRENGTH GRATITUDE

Psalm 122

A Song of degrees of David.

1 I was glad when they said unto me, Let us go into
the house of the LORD.
2 Our feet shall stand within thy gates, O Jeru-
salem.
3 Jerusalem is builded as a city that is compact
together:
4 Whither the tribes go up, the tribes of the
LORD, unto the testimony of Israel, to give thanks
unto the name of the LORD.
5 For there are set thrones of judgment, the
thrones of the house of David.
6 Pray for the peace of Jerusalem: they shall
prosper that love thee.
7 Peace be within thy walls, *and* prosperity with-
in thy palaces.
8 For my brethren and companions' sakes, I will
now say, Peace *be* within thee.
9 Because of the house of the LORD our God I will
seek thy good.

Psalm 123

A Song of degrees.

1 Unto thee lift I up mine eyes, O thou that
dwellest in the heavens.
2 Behold, as the eyes of servants *look* unto the
hand of their masters, *and* as the eyes of a maiden

unto the hand of her mistress; so our eyes *wait* upon the LORD our God, until that he have mercy upon us.
3 Have mercy upon us, O LORD, have mercy upon
us: for we are exceedingly filled with contempt.
4 Our soul is exceedingly filled with the scorning
of those that are at ease, *and* with the contempt
of the proud.

Psalm 124

A Song of degrees of David.

1 If *it had not been* the LORD who was on our side,
now may Israel say;
2 If *it had not been* the LORD who was on our side,
when men rose up against us:
3 Then they had swallowed us up quick, when
their wrath was kindled against us:
4 Then the waters had overwhelmed us, the
stream had gone over our soul:
5 Then the proud waters had gone over our soul.
6 Blessed *be* the LORD, who hath not given us *as*
a prey to their teeth.
7 Our soul is escaped as a bird out of the snare of
the fowlers: the snare is broken, and we are
escaped.
8 Our help *is* in the name of the LORD, who made
heaven and earth.

Psalm 125

A Song of degrees.

1 They that trust in the LORD *shall be* as mount
Zion, *which* cannot be removed, *but* abideth for
ever.
2 *As* the mountains *are* round about Jerusalem,
so the LORD *is* round about his people from hence-
forth even for ever.
3 For the rod of the wicked shall not rest upon
the lot of the righteous; lest the righteous put
forth their hands unto iniquity.
4 Do good, O LORD, unto *those that be* good, and
to them that are upright in their hearts.
5 As for such as turn aside unto their crooked
ways, the LORD shall lead them forth with the work-
ers of iniquity: *but* peace *shall be* upon Israel.

Psalm 126

A Song of degrees.

1 When the LORD turned again the captivity of
Zion, we were like them that dream.
2 Then was our mouth filled with laughter, and
our tongue with singing: then said they among the
heathen, The LORD hath done great things for
them.
3 The LORD hath done great things for us; *where-
of* we are glad.

REST JOY GRACE RENEWAL

4 Turn again our captivity, O LORD, as the streams
in the south.
5 They that sow in tears shall reap in joy.
6 He that goeth forth and weepeth, bearing pre-
cious seed, shall doubtless come again with rejoic-
ing, bringing his sheaves *with him.*

Psalm 127

A Song of degrees for Solomon.

1 Except the LORD build the house, they labour
in vain that build it: except the LORD keep the city,
the watchman waketh *but* in vain.
2 *It is* vain for you to rise up early, to sit up late,
to eat the bread of sorrows: *for* so he giveth his
beloved sleep.
3 Lo, children *are* an heritage of the LORD: *and*
the fruit of the womb *is his* reward.
4 As arrows *are* in the hand of a mighty man; so
are children of the youth.
5 Happy *is* the man that hath his quiver full of
them: they shall not be ashamed, but they shall
speak with the enemies in the gate.

Psalm 128

A Song of degrees.

1 Blessed *is* every one that feareth the LORD; that
walketh in his ways.

2 For thou shalt eat the labour of thine hands:
happy *shalt* thou *be*, and *it shall be* well with
thee.
3 Thy wife *shall be* as a fruitful vine by the sides of
thine house: thy children like olive plants round
about thy table.
4 Behold, that thus shall the man be blessed that
feareth the LORD.
5 The LORD shall bless thee out of Zion: and thou
shalt see the good of Jerusalem all the days of thy
life.
6 Yea, thou shalt see thy children's children, *and*
peace upon Israel.

Psalm 129

A Song of degrees.

1 Many a time have they afflicted me from my
youth, may Israel now say:
2 Many a time have they afflicted me from
my youth: yet they have not prevailed against
me.
3 The plowers plowed upon my back: they made
long their furrows.
4 The LORD *is* righteous: he hath cut asunder the
cords of the wicked.
5 Let them all be confounded and turned back
that hate Zion.

6 Let them be as the grass *upon* the housetops,
which withereth afore it groweth up:
7 Wherewith the mower filleth not his hand; nor
he that bindeth sheaves his bosom.
8 Neither do they which go by say, The blessing
of the LORD *be* upon you: we bless you in the name
of the LORD.

Psalm 130

A Song of degrees.

1 Out of the depths have I cried unto thee, O
LORD.
2 Lord, hear my voice: let thine ears be attentive
to the voice of my supplications.
3 If thou, LORD, shouldest mark iniquities, O
Lord, who shall stand?
4 But *there is* forgiveness with thee, that thou
mayest be feared.
5 I wait for the LORD, my soul doth wait, and in
his word do I hope.
6 My soul *waiteth* for the Lord more than they
that watch for the morning: *I say, more than* they
that watch for the morning.
7 Let Israel hope in the LORD: for with the LORD
there is mercy, and with him *is* plenteous redemp-
tion.
8 And he shall redeem Israel from all his iniqui-
ties.

Psalm 131

A Song of degrees of David.

1 LORD, my heart is not haughty, nor mine eyes
lofty: neither do I exercise myself in great mat-
ters, or in things too high for me.
2 Surely I have behaved and quieted myself, as a
child that is weaned of his mother: my soul *is* even
as a weaned child.
3 Let Israel hope in the LORD from henceforth
and for ever.

Psalm 132

A Song of degrees.

1 LORD, remember David, *and* all his afflictions:
2 How he sware unto the LORD, *and* vowed unto
the mighty *God* of Jacob;
3 Surely I will not come into the tabernacle of my
house, nor go up into my bed;
4 I will not give sleep to mine eyes, *or* slumber to
mine eyelids,
5 Until I find out a place for the LORD, an habita-
tion for the mighty *God* of Jacob.
6 Lo, we heard of it at Ephratah: we found it in
the fields of the wood.
7 We will go into his tabernacles: we will worship
at his footstool.
8 Arise, O LORD, into thy rest; thou, and the ark
of thy strength.

9 Let thy priests be clothed with righteousness;
and let thy saints shout for joy.
10 For thy servant David's sake turn not away the
face of thine anointed.
11 The LORD hath sworn *in* truth unto David; he
will not turn from it; Of the fruit of thy body will
I set upon thy throne.
12 If thy children will keep my covenant and my
testimony that I shall teach them, their children
shall also sit upon thy throne for evermore.
13 For the LORD hath chosen Zion; he hath
desired *it* for his habitation.
14 This *is* my rest for ever: here will I dwell; for I
have desired it.
15 I will abundantly bless her provision: I will sat-
isfy her poor with bread.
16 I will also clothe her priests with salvation: and
her saints shall shout aloud for joy.
17 There will I make the horn of David to bud: I
have ordained a lamp for mine anointed.
18 His enemies will I clothe with shame: but upon
himself shall his crown flourish.

Psalm 133

A Song of degrees of David.

1 Behold, how good and how pleasant *it is* for
brethren to dwell together in unity!

2 *It is* like the precious ointment upon the head,
that ran down upon the beard, *even* Aaron's beard:
that went down to the skirts of his garments;
3 As the dew of Hermon, *and as the dew* that
descended upon the mountains of Zion: for there
the LORD commanded the blessing, *even* life for
evermore.

Psalm 134

A Song of degrees.

1 Behold, bless ye the LORD, all *ye* servants of the
LORD, which by night stand in the house of the
LORD.
2 Lift up your hands *in* the sanctuary, and bless
the LORD.
3 The LORD that made heaven and earth bless
thee out of Zion.

Psalm 135

1 Praise ye the LORD. Praise ye the name of the
LORD; praise *him*, O ye servants of the LORD.
2 Ye that stand in the house of the LORD, in the
courts of the house of our God.
3 Praise the LORD; for the LORD *is* good: sing
praises unto his name; for *it is* pleasant.
4 For the LORD hath chosen Jacob unto himself,
and Israel for his peculiar treasure.

5 For I know that the LORD *is* great, and *that* our
Lord *is* above all gods.
6 Whatsoever the LORD pleased, *that* did he in
heaven, and in earth, in the seas, and all deep
places.
7 He causeth the vapours to ascend from the
ends of the earth; he maketh lightnings for the
rain; he bringeth the wind out of his treasuries.
8 Who smote the firstborn of Egypt, both of man
and beast.
9 *Who* sent tokens and wonders into the midst of
thee, O Egypt, upon Pharaoh, and upon all his ser-
vants.
10 Who smote great nations, and slew mighty
kings;
11 Sihon king of the Amorites, and Og king of
Bashan, and all the kingdoms of Canaan:
12 And gave their land *for* an heritage, an heritage
unto Israel his people.
13 Thy name, O LORD, *endureth* for ever; *and*
thy memorial, O LORD, throughout all genera-
tions.
14 For the LORD will judge his people, and he will
repent himself concerning his servants.
15 The idols of the heathen *are* silver and gold, the
work of men's hands.
16 They have mouths, but they speak not; eyes
have they, but they see not;

17 They have ears, but they hear not; neither is
there *any* breath in their mouths.
18 They that make them are like unto them: *so is*
every one that trusteth in them.
19 Bless the LORD, O house of Israel: bless the
LORD, O house of Aaron:
20 Bless the LORD, O house of Levi: ye that fear
the LORD, bless the LORD.
21 Blessed be the LORD out of Zion, which dwell-
eth at Jerusalem. Praise ye the LORD.

Psalm 136

1 O give thanks unto the LORD; for *he is* good: for
his mercy *endureth* for ever.
2 O give thanks unto the God of gods: for his
mercy *endureth* for ever.
3 O give thanks to the Lord of lords: for his mercy
endureth for ever.
4 To him who alone doeth great wonders: for his
mercy *endureth* for ever.
5 To him that by wisdom made the heavens: for
his mercy *endureth* for ever.
6 To him that stretched out the earth above the
waters: for his mercy *endureth* for ever.
7 To him that made great lights: for his mercy
endureth for ever:
8 The sun to rule by day: for his mercy *endureth* for
ever:

9 The moon and stars to rule by night: for his
mercy *endureth* for ever.
10 To him that smote Egypt in their firstborn: for
his mercy *endureth* for ever:
11 And brought out Israel from among them: for
his mercy *endureth* for ever:
12 With a strong hand, and with a stretched out
arm: for his mercy *endureth* for ever.
13 To him which divided the Red sea into parts:
for his mercy *endureth* for ever:
14 And made Israel to pass through the midst of
it: for his mercy *endureth* for ever:
15 But overthrew Pharaoh and his host in the Red
sea: for his mercy *endureth* for ever.
16 To him which led his people through the wil-
derness: for his mercy *endureth* for ever.
17 To him which smote great kings: for his mercy
endureth for ever:
18 And slew famous kings: for his mercy *endureth*
for ever:
19 Sihon king of the Amorites: for his mercy
endureth for ever:
20 And Og the king of Bashan: for his mercy
endureth for ever:
21 And gave their land for an heritage: for his
mercy *endureth* for ever:
22 *Even* an heritage unto Israel his servant: for his
mercy *endureth* for ever.

23 Who remembered us in our low estate: for his
mercy *endureth* for ever:
24 And hath redeemed us from our enemies: for
his mercy *endureth* for ever.
25 Who giveth food to all flesh: for his mercy
endureth for ever.
26 O give thanks unto the God of heaven: for his
mercy *endureth* for ever.

Psalm 137

1 By the rivers of Babylon, there we sat down,
yea, we wept, when we remembered Zion.
2 We hanged our harps upon the willows in the
midst thereof.
3 For there they that carried us away captive
required of us a song; and they that wasted us
required of us mirth, *saying,* Sing us *one* of the
songs of Zion.
4 How shall we sing the LORD'S song in a strange
land?
5 If I forget thee, O Jerusalem, let my right hand
forget *her cunning.*
6 If I do not remember thee, let my tongue cleave
to the roof of my mouth; if I prefer not Jerusalem
above my chief joy.
7 Remember, O LORD, the children of Edom in
the day of Jerusalem; who said, Rase *it,* rase *it,*
even to the foundation thereof.

8 O daughter of Babylon, who art to be destroyed;
happy *shall he be*, that rewardeth thee as thou hast
served us.
9 Happy *shall he be*, that taketh and dasheth thy
little ones against the stones.

Psalm 138

A Psalm *of David*.

1 I will praise thee with my whole heart: before
the gods will I sing praise unto thee.
2 I will worship toward thy holy temple, and praise
thy name for thy lovingkindness and for thy truth:
for thou hast magnified thy word above all thy
name.
3 In the day when I cried thou answeredst me,
and strengthenedst me *with* strength in my
soul.
4 All the kings of the earth shall praise thee, O
LORD, when they hear the words of thy mouth.
5 Yea, they shall sing in the ways of the LORD: for
great *is* the glory of the LORD.
6 Though the LORD *be* high, yet hath he respect
unto the lowly: but the proud he knoweth afar
off.
7 Though I walk in the midst of trouble, thou wilt
revive me: thou shalt stretch forth thine hand
against the wrath of mine enemies, and thy right
hand shall save me.

PEACE COMFORT HOPE STRENGTH GRATITUDE

8 The LORD will perfect *that which* concerneth
me: thy mercy, O LORD, *endureth* for ever: for-
sake not the works of thine own hands.

Psalm 139

To the chief Musician, A Psalm of David.

1 O LORD, thou hast searched me, and known
me.
2 Thou knowest my downsitting and mine upris-
ing, thou understandest my thought afar off.
3 Thou compassest my path and my lying down,
and art acquainted *with* all my ways.
4 For *there is* not a word in my tongue, *but*, lo, O
LORD, thou knowest it altogether.
5 Thou hast beset me behind and before, and laid
thine hand upon me.
6 *Such* knowledge *is* too wonderful for me; it is
high, I cannot *attain* unto it.
7 Whither shall I go from thy spirit? or whither
shall I flee from thy presence?
8 If I ascend up into heaven, thou *art* there: if I
make my bed in hell, behold, thou *art there.*
9 *If* I take the wings of the morning, *and* dwell in
the uttermost parts of the sea;
10 Even there shall thy hand lead me, and thy
right hand shall hold me.
11 If I say, Surely the darkness shall cover me;
even the night shall be light about me.

REST JOY GRACE RENEWAL

12 Yea, the darkness hideth not from thee; but
the night shineth as the day: the darkness and the
light *are* both alike *to thee.*
13 For thou hast possessed my reins: thou hast
covered me in my mother's womb.
14 I will praise thee; for I am fearfully *and* won-
derfully made: marvellous *are* thy works; and *that*
my soul knoweth right well.
15 My substance was not hid from thee, when I
was made in secret, *and* curiously wrought in the
lowest parts of the earth.
16 Thine eyes did see my substance, yet being
unperfect; and in thy book all *my members* were
written, *which* in continuance were fashioned,
when *as yet there was* none of them.
17 How precious also are thy thoughts unto me,
O God! how great is the sum of them!
18 *If* I should count them, they are more in num-
ber than the sand: when I awake, I am still with
thee.
19 Surely thou wilt slay the wicked, O God: depart
from me therefore, ye bloody men.
20 For they speak against thee wickedly, *and*
thine enemies take *thy name* in vain.
21 Do not I hate them, O LORD, that hate thee? and
am not I grieved with those that rise up against thee?
22 I hate them with perfect hatred: I count them
mine enemies.

23 Search me, O God, and know my heart: try
me, and know my thoughts:
24 And see if *there be any* wicked way in me, and
lead me in the way everlasting.

Psalm 140

To the chief Musician, A Psalm of David.

1 Deliver me, O LORD, from the evil man: pre-
serve me from the violent man;
2 Which imagine mischiefs in *their* heart; contin-
ually are they gathered together *for* war.
3 They have sharpened their tongues like a ser-
pent; adders' poison *is* under their lips. Selah.
4 Keep me, O LORD, from the hands of the wick-
ed; preserve me from the violent man; who have
purposed to overthrow my goings.
5 The proud have hid a snare for me, and cords;
they have spread a net by the wayside; they have
set gins for me. Selah.
6 I said unto the LORD, Thou *art* my God: hear the
voice of my supplications, O LORD.
7 O GOD the Lord, the strength of my salvation,
thou hast covered my head in the day of battle.
8 Grant not, O LORD, the desires of the wicked:
further not his wicked device; *lest* they exalt them-
selves. Selah.
9 *As for* the head of those that compass me about,
let the mischief of their own lips cover them.

REST JOY GRACE RENEWAL

10 Let burning coals fall upon them: let them be
cast into the fire; into deep pits, that they rise not
up again.
11 Let not an evil speaker be established in the
earth: evil shall hunt the violent man to overthrow
him.
12 I know that the LORD will maintain the cause
of the afflicted, *and* the right of the poor.
13 Surely the righteous shall give thanks unto thy
name: the upright shall dwell in thy presence.

Psalm 141

A Psalm of David.

1 LORD, I cry unto thee: make haste unto me; give
ear unto my voice, when I cry unto thee.
2 Let my prayer be set forth before thee *as*
incense; *and* the lifting up of my hands *as* the eve-
ning sacrifice.
3 Set a watch, O LORD, before my mouth; keep
the door of my lips.
4 Incline not my heart to *any* evil thing, to prac-
tise wicked works with men that work iniquity: and
let me not eat of their dainties.
5 Let the righteous smite me; *it shall be* a kindness:
and let him reprove me; *it shall be* an excellent oil,
which shall not break my head: for yet my prayer
also *shall be* in their calamities.

6 When their judges are overthrown in stony
places, they shall hear my words; for they are
sweet.
7 Our bones are scattered at the grave's mouth,
as when one cutteth and cleaveth *wood* upon the
earth.
8 But mine eyes *are* unto thee, O GOD the Lord:
in thee is my trust; leave not my soul destitute.
9 Keep me from the snares *which* they have laid
for me, and the gins of the workers of iniquity.
10 Let the wicked fall into their own nets, whilst
that I withal escape.

Psalm 142

Maschil of David; A Prayer when he was in the cave.

1 I cried unto the LORD with my voice; with my
voice unto the LORD did I make my supplication.
2 I poured out my complaint before him; I shewed
before him my trouble.
3 When my spirit was overwhelmed within me,
then thou knewest my path. In the way wherein I
walked have they privily laid a snare for me.
4 I looked on *my* right hand, and beheld, but *there*
was no man that would know me: refuge failed me;
no man cared for my soul.
5 I cried unto thee, O LORD: I said, Thou *art* my
refuge *and* my portion in the land of the living.

6 Attend unto my cry; for I am brought very low:
deliver me from my persecutors; for they are stron-
ger than I.
7 Bring my soul out of prison, that I may praise
thy name: the righteous shall compass me about;
for thou shalt deal bountifully with me.

Psalm 143

A Psalm of David.

1 Hear my prayer, O LORD, give ear to my sup-
plications: in thy faithfulness answer me, *and* in
thy righteousness.
2 And enter not into judgment with thy servant:
for in thy sight shall no man living be justified.
3 For the enemy hath persecuted my soul; he
hath smitten my life down to the ground; he hath
made me to dwell in darkness, as those that have
been long dead.
4 Therefore is my spirit overwhelmed within me;
my heart within me is desolate.
5 I remember the days of old; I meditate on all
thy works; I muse on the work of thy hands.
6 I stretch forth my hands unto thee: my soul
thirsteth after thee, as a thirsty land. Selah.
7 Hear me speedily, O LORD: my spirit faileth:
hide not thy face from me, lest I be like unto them
that go down into the pit.

8 Cause me to hear thy lovingkindness in the
morning; for in thee do I trust: cause me to know
the way wherein I should walk; for I lift up my soul
unto thee.
9 Deliver me, O LORD, from mine enemies: I flee
unto thee to hide me.
10 Teach me to do thy will; for thou *art* my God:
thy spirit *is* good; lead me into the land of upright-
ness.
11 Quicken me, O LORD, for thy name's sake: for thy
righteousness' sake bring my soul out of trouble.
12 And of thy mercy cut off mine enemies, and
destroy all them that afflict my soul: for I *am* thy
servant.

Psalm 144

A Psalm *of David.*

1 Blessed *be* the LORD my strength which
teacheth my hands to war, *and* my fingers to fight:
2 My goodness, and my fortress; my high tower,
and my deliverer; my shield, and *he* in whom I
trust; who subdueth my people under me.
3 LORD, what *is* man, that thou takest knowledge
of him! *or* the son of man, that thou makest
account of him!
4 Man is like to vanity: his days *are* as a shadow
that passeth away.

5 Bow thy heavens, O LORD, and come down:
touch the mountains, and they shall smoke.
6 Cast forth lightning, and scatter them: shoot
out thine arrows, and destroy them.
7 Send thine hand from above; rid me, and deliv-
er me out of great waters, from the hand of
strange children;
8 Whose mouth speaketh vanity, and their right
hand *is* a right hand of falsehood.
9 I will sing a new song unto thee, O God: upon a
psaltery *and* an instrument of ten strings will I sing
praises unto thee.
10 *It is he* that giveth salvation unto kings: who
delivereth David his servant from the hurtful
sword.
11 Rid me, and deliver me from the hand of
strange children, whose mouth speaketh vanity,
and their right hand *is* a right hand of falsehood:
12 That our sons *may be* as plants grown up in their
youth; *that* our daughters *may be* as corner stones,
polished *after* the similitude of a palace:
13 *That* our garners *may be* full, affording all man-
ner of store: *that* our sheep may bring forth thou-
sands and ten thousands in our streets:
14 *That* our oxen *may be* strong to labour; *that*
there be no breaking in, nor going out; that *there*
be no complaining in our streets.

15 Happy *is that* people, that is in such a case: *yea,*
happy *is that* people, whose God *is* the LORD.

Psalm 145

David's Psalm *of praise.*

1 I will extol thee, my God, O king; and I will bless
thy name for ever and ever.
2 Every day will I bless thee; and I will praise thy
name for ever and ever.
3 Great *is* the LORD, and greatly to be praised;
and his greatness *is* unsearchable.
4 One generation shall praise thy works to anoth-
er, and shall declare thy mighty acts.
5 I will speak of the glorious honour of thy maj-
esty, and of thy wondrous works.
6 And *men* shall speak of the might of thy terri-
ble acts: and I will declare thy greatness.
7 They shall abundantly utter the memory of thy
great goodness, and shall sing of thy righteousness.
8 The LORD *is* gracious, and full of compassion;
slow to anger, and of great mercy.
9 The LORD *is* good to all: and his tender mercies
are over all his works.
10 All thy works shall praise thee, O LORD; and
thy saints shall bless thee.
11 They shall speak of the glory of thy kingdom,
and talk of thy power;

REST JOY GRACE RENEWAL

12 To make known to the sons of men his mighty
acts, and the glorious majesty of his kingdom.
13 Thy kingdom *is* an everlasting kingdom, and thy
dominion *endureth* throughout all generations.
14 The LORD upholdeth all that fall, and raiseth up
all *those that be* bowed down.
15 The eyes of all wait upon thee; and thou givest
them their meat in due season.
16 Thou openest thine hand, and satisfiest the
desire of every living thing.
17 The LORD *is* righteous in all his ways, and holy
in all his works.
18 The LORD *is* nigh unto all them that call upon
him, to all that call upon him in truth.
19 He will fulfil the desire of them that fear him:
he also will hear their cry, and will save them.
20 The LORD preserveth all them that love him:
but all the wicked will he destroy.
21 My mouth shall speak the praise of the LORD:
and let all flesh bless his holy name for ever and
ever.

Psalm 146

1 Praise ye the LORD. Praise the LORD, O my soul.
2 While I live will I praise the LORD: I will sing
praises unto my God while I have any being.
3 Put not your trust in princes, *nor* in the son of
man, in whom *there is* no help.

4 His breath goeth forth, he returneth to his
earth; in that very day his thoughts perish.
5 Happy *is he* that *hath* the God of Jacob for his
help, whose hope *is* in the LORD his God:
6 Which made heaven, and earth, the sea, and all
that therein *is*: which keepeth truth for ever:
7 Which executeth judgment for the oppressed:
which giveth food to the hungry. The LORD
looseth the prisoners:
8 The LORD openeth *the eyes of* the blind: the
LORD raiseth them that are bowed down: the
LORD loveth the righteous:
9 The LORD preserveth the strangers; he reliev-
eth the fatherless and widow: but the way of the
wicked he turneth upside down.
10 The LORD shall reign for ever, *even* thy God, O
Zion, unto all generations. Praise ye the LORD.

Psalm 147

1 Praise ye the LORD: for *it is* good to sing praises
unto our God; for *it is* pleasant; *and* praise is
comely.
2 The LORD doth build up Jerusalem: he gath-
ereth together the outcasts of Israel.
3 He healeth the broken in heart, and bindeth up
their wounds.
4 He telleth the number of the stars; he calleth
them all by *their* names.

REST JOY GRACE RENEWAL

5 Great *is* our Lord, and of great power: his
understanding *is* infinite.
6 The LORD lifteth up the meek: he casteth the
wicked down to the ground.
7 Sing unto the LORD with thanksgiving; sing
praise upon the harp unto our God:
8 Who covereth the heaven with clouds, who
prepareth rain for the earth, who maketh grass to
grow upon the mountains.
9 He giveth to the beast his food, *and* to the
young ravens which cry.
10 He delighteth not in the strength of the horse:
he taketh not pleasure in the legs of a man.
11 The LORD taketh pleasure in them that fear
him, in those that hope in his mercy.
12 Praise the LORD, O Jerusalem; praise thy God,
O Zion.
13 For he hath strengthened the bars of thy gates;
he hath blessed thy children within thee.
14 He maketh peace *in* thy borders, *and* filleth
thee with the finest of the wheat.
15 He sendeth forth his commandment *upon*
earth: his word runneth very swiftly.
16 He giveth snow like wool: he scattereth the
hoarfrost like ashes.
17 He casteth forth his ice like morsels: who can
stand before his cold?

PEACE COMFORT HOPE STRENGTH GRATITUDE

18 He sendeth out his word, and melteth them:
he causeth his wind to blow, *and* the waters flow.
19 He sheweth his word unto Jacob, his statutes
and his judgments unto Israel.
20 He hath not dealt so with any nation: and *as*
for his judgments, they have not known them.
Praise ye the LORD.

Psalm 148

1 Praise ye the LORD. Praise ye the LORD from the
heavens: praise him in the heights.
2 Praise ye him, all his angels: praise ye him, all
his hosts.
3 Praise ye him, sun and moon: praise him, all ye
stars of light.
4 Praise him, ye heavens of heavens, and ye
waters that *be* above the heavens.
5 Let them praise the name of the LORD: for he
commanded, and they were created.
6 He hath also stablished them for ever and ever:
he hath made a decree which shall not pass.
7 Praise the LORD from the earth, ye dragons, and
all deeps:
8 Fire, and hail; snow, and vapours; stormy wind
fulfilling his word:
9 Mountains, and all hills; fruitful trees, and all
cedars:

10 Beasts, and all cattle; creeping things, and fly-
ing fowl:
11 Kings of the earth, and all people; princes, and
all judges of the earth:
12 Both young men, and maidens; old men, and
children:
13 Let them praise the name of the LORD: for his
name alone is excellent; his glory *is* above the
earth and heaven.
14 He also exalteth the horn of his people, the
praise of all his saints; *even* of the children of Isra-
el, a people near unto him. Praise ye the LORD.

Psalm 149

1 Praise ye the LORD. Sing unto the LORD a new
song, *and* his praise in the congregation of saints.
2 Let Israel rejoice in him that made him: let the
children of Zion be joyful in their King.
3 Let them praise his name in the dance: let them
sing praises unto him with the timbrel and harp.
4 For the LORD taketh pleasure in his people: he
will beautify the meek with salvation.
5 Let the saints be joyful in glory: let them sing
aloud upon their beds.
6 *Let* the high *praises* of God *be* in their mouth,
and a two-edged sword in their hand;
7 To execute vengeance upon the heathen, *and*
punishments upon the people;

8 To bind their kings with chains, and their nobles
with fetters of iron;
9 To execute upon them the judgment written:
this honour have all his saints. Praise ye the LORD.

Psalm 150

1 Praise ye the LORD. Praise God in his sanctu-
ary: praise him in the firmament of his power.
2 Praise him for his mighty acts: praise him
according to his excellent greatness.
3 Praise him with the sound of the trumpet:
praise him with the psaltery and harp.
4 Praise him with the timbrel and dance: praise
him with stringed instruments and organs.
5 Praise him upon the loud cymbals: praise him
upon the high sounding cymbals.
6 Let every thing that hath breath praise the
LORD. Praise ye the LORD.

SCRIPTURE INDEX
FOR THE NINE THEMES FOUND IN THIS EDITION

Comfort

Grace

Gratitude

Hope

Renewal

Rest

Strength

DaySpring

Dear Friend,

This book of Psalms was published with you in mind, and we pray it will encourage you right where you are. At DaySpring, our vision is to see every person experience the life-changing message of God's love, not just on Sundays, but every day of the week. As we worked through creating each feature—from choosing the translation, to designing the cover, even to selecting the type of binding—we prayed for you to encounter His unfailing love and indescribable peace within its pages. It is our hope that this book of Psalms doesn't only fill your head with knowledge but strengthens your connection with and understanding of God.

THE DAYSPRING BIBLE TEAM